FINANCIAL GENIUS

by

Mark Oliver Haroldsen

Mark O. Haroldsen, Inc.   Salt Lake City, Utah

Printed in the United States of America

Revised Edition 1984

Published and distributed by Mark O. Haroldsen, Inc.
Marko Plaza
1831 Fort Union Blvd.,
Salt Lake City, Utah 84121

FOREWORD

When I was 25 years old, my wife and I, while living in Denver, found ourselves in a desperate financial situation. I had just lost my job and my wife was expecting our second child and we hadn't a dime's worth of insurance to cover it. We even had to borrow money from my father and father-in-law in order to pay the rent and bills and buy a few groceries for the two of us and our one year old son.

It was then that I determined never to suffer this way again, and even at the time when everything seemed hopeless, I was presumptious enough to dream and scheme and set my goals to become a millionaire. I said to myself—and even had the gall to write it down—that by the time I was 30, I would retire. The fact is well documented now that six short years later, I had achieved that goal.

A year later in 1976, I wrote and published a book about what I had done to achieve my financial independence. The book is entitled *How to Wake Up the Financial Genius Inside You* and has sold over 1,000,000 copies.

At this printing, I have completely revised and updated this book to make it more applicable to the real estate market today. Real estate investment is the tool I've found to be most beneficial and suitable to achieving my goals.

Many people have felt that I make my money through the sale of my book and the result of the publication of the nationwide magazine, *The Financial Freedom Report.* I'm not at all embarassed to state that I've done very well from the proceeds of the sales of these two publications. However, my personal focus is real estate investment and here is a little recap of what has happened since the first printing of *How to Wake Up the Financial Genius Inside You,* in 1976. Prior to publishing the book, through the purchase of real estate, my net worth had risen to over a million dollars during my 31st year. For the next year, I concentrated on getting my book published, starting up my magazine, the *Financial Freedom Report,* and launching a nationwide seminar program. In late 1977, I renewed my effort to acquire property; and then something happened that I had not counted upon, which was a pleasant surprise. The many thousands of people in that period of time that had purchased my book and subsequently subscribed to my magazine and attended my seminars, began sending to me the deals they could not handle. Having a healthy net worth and some cash to work with, I was able to make bargain purchases of property all over the country. Since that time I have purchased property in North Carolina, Pennsylvania, Illinois, Idaho, and of course, Utah. These have been major multi-million dollar purchases that have greatly enhanced my investor position. One of the projects has been successfully converted into condominiums, bringing in over a million dollars in profit.

If someone were to ask me today what success has done to change me, I would have to say the major area of change has been the great appreciation I have for time, and the great part it plays in achieving our goals through good utilization of it, and also the using of other people's talents. I've been able to achieve much more than I could have alone.

Also, the greatest realization that I have come to, and that I regularly expound, is that if I could do it, so can you. Success is a process; it is not an end result, for there are greater and greater successes awaiting those who apply for themselves the success principles of planning, following a game plan, and sticking to the financial goals that you've set for yourself. Do this and you'll wake up the FINANCIAL GENIUS inside you.

ACKNOWLEDGMENTS

I acknowledge all those men and women throughout the world who are self-made millionaires. I acknowledge you, the reader, for taking the time and trouble to buy and read this book. That time and effort sets you apart from the majority, and you are one who *can* succeed in the ambition to make a million.

Remember: the mere reading will only give you direction. It will give you a solid formula and specific recipes for success. But you must act and follow those directions. As you do, you will not only prosper financially, but you will learn a wealth of information about this financial endeavor that will allow you to give directions to others who can follow your example and act on your direction.

Special Thanks

To those who have put so much time effort in to editing and connecting this and past editions—to Vicki Williams who years ago edited my 1st rough (very rough) draft to Virginia Facknell who spent countless hours using her great skills to improve the first edition and more recently thanks to Mike Hansen, Carolyn Tice, Craig Steed, who have contributed much and a special thanks to Connie Smith for helping update this last edition.

PREFACE

Sometime ago I spent a long session with a great man whom I admire. This man has reached great heights. Financially, he is a millionaire, but that is just the beginning. Religiously, he is one of the top leaders of the rapidly growing Mormon Church. In addition, he was a leader for many years in a major multibillion-dollar industry. He is highly thought of, and is truly a top-notch businessman and salesman. The author of many books, he has been heard on radio and television hundreds of times.

A large investor, he has been in everything from real estate to stocks and bonds, and many things in between. He has also backed many young, ambitious men in their private ventures. He is truly a grand, old gentleman who has the energy and enthusiasm of a man one half his age.

During our session, I asked him for his secret for success. He answered that when he was quite young he decided if he wanted to be a great man, achieve much, and reach the height of success, he would have to know what the great men of the world thought. He set upon the task of reading about the great men of the world, reading the words they had written, and then re-thinking each of their thoughts in an attempt to make their great thoughts his own. From each one he attempted to find something of benefit. Next, he made a habit of always carrying two books, one to read from and one to write in. As he read great thoughts, he would write down his own thoughts that were stimulated by the reading. Later, he published many of his thoughts into his own books.

What I learned from this great man is that probably the shortest route a person can take in the quest for excellence and struggle for financial success is to study thoroughly the great men and their lives. I began to study the great financial fortunes of the world, the men who made those fortunes, and how they did it. I investigated their thoughts, read the principles, formulas, and recipes they felt were important, discovered their thought processes, gained insight from their personal habits, benefited from their experience, and saw how they actually made their millions.

Contained in this book are both a summary of what I learned from these great men and also how it changed my life and financial condition through the general laws of success applied to a specific formula for accumulation of wealth.

HOW TO READ THIS BOOK

At the end of each chapter, there are blank pages entitled "Notes and Thoughts." These pages are for you to write your thoughts, ideas, and goals. Do not write my thoughts; write the thoughts that are stimulated in your mind from reading my comments.

You will find as you read this book, particularly the second and third times, that your own ideas multiply. Consequently, you will find yourself writing many of your own great thoughts.

My task is not only to show you the formulas and methods that will lead you to success, but also to stimulate your mind and bring out great thoughts and ideas that are and always have been in your mind. Those thoughts, along with a little direction and guidance that will help you form a game plan, will bring rewards and riches you once thought came only to others.

CONTENTS

CHAPTER 1

MAKING MILLIONS FROM PENNIES

If I gave you a choice of working for me for $1,000 a day for a period of thirty-five days, versus working for yourself for one cent the first day and doubling the amount each day for thirty-five days, which job offer would you take?

Obviously, if you were to take the first choice, at the end of thirty-five days you would have $35,000. A wage of $35,000 in thirty-five days is phenomenal. Had you chosen the alternative of working for one cent the first day and doubling the amount each day for thirty-five days, you would be compounding your money at 100 percent per day.

When I use this example in lectures, usually about half the people prefer the first job offer and half the second. Without the aid of a pencil or calculator, decide which choice you would make.

OFFER 1		OFFER 2	
	Amount in		**Amount in**
Day	**Dollars**	**Day**	**Dollars**
1	$1,000	1	$ .01
2	1,000	2	.02
3	1,000	3	.04
4	1,000	4	.08
5	1,000	5	.16
6	1,000	6	.32
7	1,000	7	.64
8	1,000	8	1.28
	$8,000		$2.55

Have you made a decision yet? Would you take the sure $1,000 per day, or 100 percent compounded from a beginning penny?

Total Days 1-8 $2.55

OFFER 1

Day	Amount in Dollars
9	$ 1,000
10	1,000
11	1,000
12	1,000
13	1,000
14	1,000
15	1,000
16	1,000
	$16,000

OFFER 2

Day	Amount in Dollars
9	$ 2.55
10	5.10
11	10.20
12	20.40
13	40.80
14	81.60
15	163.20
16	326.40
	$652.80

How about now? Which choice do you favor?

Total Days 1-16 $652.80

OFFER 1

Day	Amount in Dollars
17	$ 1,000
18	1,000
19	1,000
20	1,000
21	1,000
22	1,000
23	1,000
24	1,000
	$24,000

OFFER 2

Day	Amount in Dollars
17	$ 650.00
18	1,300.00
19	2,600.00
20	5,200.00
21	10,400.00
22	20,800.00
23	41,600.00
24	83,200.00
	$166,402.80

Not much of a problem to decide now. And you have eleven days to let your money grow.

Total Days 1-24 $166,402.80

| OFFER 1 | | OFFER 2 | |
Day	Amount in Dollars	Day	Amount in Dollars
25	$ 1,000	25	$ 165,750.00
26	1,000	26	331,500.00
27	1,000	27	663,000.00
28	1,000	28	1,326,000.00
29	1,000	29	2,652,000.00
30	1,000	30	5,304,000.00
31	1,000	31	10,608,000.00
32	1,000	32	21,216,000.00
33	1,000	33	42,432,000.00
34	1,000	34	84,864,000.00
35	1,000	35	169,728,000.00
	$35,000		$339,456,652.80

Note: These figures have been rounded off for ease of calculating.

Most people find it almost impossible to believe that one penny compounded at 100 percent per day is worth over a third of a billion dollars on the thirty-fifth day.

Sure, that is an exaggerated example of the fantastic effects of compounding interest, but the use of compound interest is virtually the only way to make millions today. Try changing days to years (more on that later).

LEVERAGE MAKES YOUR MONEY WORK HARDER

I was extremely fortunate in that I was given some good advice early in my career. A man of great wealth told me to get to know and fully comprehend interest rates, leverage, and how to compound investment capital through good investments. Although his advice did not sink in at that time and he did not elaborate on the types of investments to make, a few years later when I started making small investments, what he had said came back to me. And the results from using his philosophy have been amazing.

As with many young men, my goal had always been to become a millionaire. Like most, I became frustrated. I worked hard, but there didn't seem to be enough hours in the day to make a million. I reasoned that there had to be a way; I knew people who had achieved that goal, many of them still young. I studied the lives of more than two dozen millionaires and finally realized that the only practical way of making a million was to have your money work as hard for you as you work for yourself. Later I learned that with the wise use of leverage your money can literally work ten times harder than you can. I was on the way! The next step was to learn as much as I could about money, interest rates, and the use of leverage and compounding.

Even though I was busy at the time, I took time out to really learn and understand everything there was to know about the compounding of money. I particularly focused on the wise use of leverage. What leverage could do for you and to you astounded me. It has to be the most incredible tool in this era of inflation.

Virtually all of the financial wizards, industrial giants, and self-made millionaires now and in times past have realized the profound effect of the compounding of money.

SIMPLE COMPOUNDING
Compounding, of course, simply means that you earn

interest on top of interest. For example, if you invest $1,000 for one year at 15 percent return, at the end of the first year you have $1,150, or 15 percent over and above the amount you started with. Your profit is $150.

The second year the entire $1,150 would earn at the rate of 15 percent for a total of $172.50 interest. This $172.50 interest added to the $1,150 brings your total to $1,322.50.

Whereas money experts agree that it is not realistic to compound money at 100 percent per day for thirty-five days, as in our example, most would agree that it is possible to compound money at 100 percent per year for thirty-five years. It is possible, and indeed not difficult, to compound money at 30 percent per year. In fact, there are many examples, including my own, where people have compounded their assets at over 100 percent per year. In Chapters 6 and 7 on leverage, you will see how easily this can be done on sums as low as a couple hundred dollars, and on several hundred thousand dollars. This is less difficult to accomplish in the early years of an investment program when you are not dealing with large amounts of capital.

Even with the less dramatic figure of 30 percent, the results are amazing. For example, when $10,000 is compounded at 30 percent for eighteen years, the result is an accumulation of capital in excess of $1,124,000. Would it surprise you to know that many people compound their assets at the rate of 30 percent per year, particularly those with a net worth of less than $1 million? In Chapter 6 you will find out exactly how to consistently compound your money at 30 percent (and higher!).

Even though I felt I knew and understood interest rates, compounding, and how to use leverage, at that point I lacked the proper investments to try out my new-found knowledge. I tried stocks and bonds (in fact, I used a $1,500 government-backed school loan to experiment), only to find that because I lacked control over the investment I consistently lost money.

I thought some control could be gained if I were closer to the investment, so I joined a stock brokerage firm, and lost more money. It was then, as a stock broker, that I found the type of investment that could give me a consistent, dependable, and at the same time, a high return.

THERE HAD TO BE A "GOLDEN GOOSE"

While trying to get my feet wet as a young, green-as-grass stock broker for Paine, Webber, Jackson and Curtis, I met a client (an account I inherited when a broker left the firm) who showed me what I had been searching for.

Larry Rosenberg worked as an accountant for the Public Service of Colorado. He used to call for stock quotes; and once in a while he would buy 400 or 500 shares of a stock. At first I couldn't figure out where he was getting all the money. (His stock picks weren't bad, but nothing great.) I knew he couldn't be getting it from his salary, so I concluded he had either inherited it or was embezzling!

I finally got up the nerve to ask Larry what and where his "golden goose" was. He told me it was apartments in northeast Denver. The real shocker was the number of apartments he owned, and where and how he started.

Mr. Rosenberg not only had acquired more than a thousand units, but he had started with nothing only twelve years before. He did it in a part of Denver that was going downhill. Larry and his brother, Lew, have not only made themselves a fortune, but they have made a great contribution to an entire section of Denver. They have improved and upgraded buildings and grounds to the advantage of everyone.

I had found an investment I could control, one where I could apply leverage and compounding. I was excited because I could begin immediately by buying small units.

HIGH RATES OF RETURN

If you are a small investor or just beginning, you really have a big advantage in many areas of investing. Whether you are shooting for a rate of return of 15 percent, 30 percent, 50 percent, or 100 percent, you can compound your money at these higher rates more easily because of the amount of money you are working with. The reason is that many large investors are not interested in some of the areas that you as a small investor are interested in. Consequently, while you still have small sums to invest, you can increase your average annual return dramatically.

For example, you can invest in a small real estate property — a duplex, four-plex, ten units, or thereabouts, where your only competitors in buying such units are people in similar situations, people without a lot of capital. Additionally, these people don't generally have a vast amount of experience or knowledge, so with a little extra effort you can surpass your competition.

Later, as your assets begin to build to around $800,000 or $900,000 you will find it harder to get the higher return every year. However, another thing will happen at this point — your abilities as an owner and investor will have compounded and it will be possible to continue at a high rate of return. The point is that your brain actually has a similar power to compound itself. In "Can Exercise Improve Your Brain Power?" *Reader's Digest,* May 1973, the author (Edwin Diamond) indicated that through physical and mental exercise your brain size can actually increase.

Each of us begins life with roughly ten billion brain cells. There are literally tens of billions of connective glia cells that can increase the size of the brain and the mental capacity of the person who does those things to stimulate or "compound" it.

Conversely, a person who does not exercise both brain and body, but who does the same things every day and stays in a narrow routine, becomes less alert and his brain power diminishes, or at best stays the same. As one broadens his horizons and packs many and varied experiences into his life, he finds that a compounding effect takes place — the more he learns the more he wants to learn; in fact, the easier it is to learn. The more experience one has the more he wants to have, and he finds it easier to comprehend and benefit by these added experiences. I call this brain compounding. It is just as important as money compounding, and the two principles should be used jointly. It was said of J.P. Morgan that he had the genius to focus all of his mental powers and concentrate on one thing for five minutes.

REAL ESTATE AND BRAIN COMPOUNDING

Let me give you an example of combining the two types of compounding. I had been building my asset base slowly for a little over a year. At the same time my mental abilities, at least when focused on investments, began to compound. A real estate agent through whom I had bought several properties came to me all excited about a fantastic little investment he had found.

My first question: "Why don't you buy it if it's so great?" He brushed this aside, saying he was too old to get involved in buying single family houses.

bought several properties came to me all excited about a fantastic little investment in a single family house.

I told him that single family units were not in my game plan and that I didn't have any extra investment cash. He insisted on showing me the house. I went along out of curiosity and was surprised to find a modest, well-kept home in a lower income area in tip-top condition. It was obviously worth the $14,500 asking price. But the Realtor had described it as a "fantastic bargain." Sure enough, the seller's wife said they had to sell it that week and were lowering the price to $10,000. Within an hour I had written an offer to buy it for $10,000 cash.

I made the offer with less than $500 in the bank. But my brain had been working fast from the moment I saw the house. I wasn't going to let that bargain slip through my fingers. I was sure I could borrow the money somewhere. If I couldn't, I would only lose $100 earnest money. The odds were attractive.

The minute I had the seller's signature I went directly to the largest bank in town. Because my credit was good, I secured a $10,000 loan on my signature. Two days later I picked up the money, went to the closing, paid the money, and took title to one of the few properties I have ever owned free and clear. But that state of affairs didn't last long. I went to another bank with which I had been dealing for some time and asked for a long-term real estate loan on the property. Within three weeks they had appraised the property and loaned me $10,000, which was 70 percent of their appraised value (a low appraisal, incidentally).

Of course, I took the $10,000 from the mortgage money and paid off the first bank. My wonderful tenants were now paying off the mortgage. After all expenses were paid, more than $700 was left over each year. That extra income was tax free (see Chapter 13), and with inflation the house was eventually worth several times what I paid for it.

In the chapters on leverage, you will find several other examples of this type of leverage and financing with much larger properties.

This example has two points: (1) In spite of prevailing market conditions you can find attractive rates of return and make your money compound quickly. In this example you can't even determine the percentage rate of return on my initial investment, since I really didn't have anything invested in the property. And (2), if you are actively engaged in seeking investments and comparing financial data, appraisals, and methods of financing, your mind works overtime and starts to compound. You think of ways of getting the job done that never would have crossed your mind earlier. This is brain compounding.

FORMULA FOR MILLIONS
AND MULTIMILLIONS

There are many high-powered, complex formulas for success and financial independence, most of which are so mind boggling it would take a Ph.D. to understand them and a Phi Beta Kappa to interpret. Many of these formulas were written by people who never actually made it themselves but sat back and watched others do it.

From a spectator position they think they know the answers and make things so complex and involved that the average person cannot understand them. Take it from me, making a lot of money in a short period of time can be done with a simple game plan. I like the slogan used by Charlie "Tremendous" Jones in his books and lectures. It is "SIB-KIS" — See It Big, Keep It Simple. As he puts it,

most of us see something small and then make it complex
so that nobody else can understand it. (Charles E.
Jones, *Life Is Tremendous* [Wheaton, Illinois: Tyndale House
Publishers, 1968], pp. 15-17.)

When I studied the lives and fortunes of the two
dozen millionaires, I was looking for a common
denominator: Something they all had or did that ac-
counted for their success. I finally noticed factors that
were present in almost every fortune. I slowly eliminated
those factors that didn't show up in every case. What I
ended up with was basic and somewhat obvious, although
it escapes 96 percent of those who look for it.

FINANCIAL SUCCESS = P + S + I + C

There are four essential ingredients, and I put them
into a formula: PSIC, which simply translates into P =
Plan, S = Save, I = Invest, C = Compound.

A man by the name of Owen Feltham said, "The
greatest results in life are usually attained by simple means
and the exercise of ordinary qualities. These may for the
most part be summed in these two words — common
sense and perseverance." I assume you have common
sense and that you will persevere. I also assume that you
have a certain amount of motivation or you would not be
reading this book. Two other essential ingredients to make
the PSIC formula work are drive and desire. These two
qualities can be learned and added upon.

Motivation, drive, and desire can overcome many
handicaps. However, without technical and practical
knowledge of how to make money, a person can work
hard and still be unfruitful and unproductive. Without
motivation, all of the formulas, practical methods, and
game plans in the world are not worth twenty-seven cents.

The object of this book is to provide both the stimulus to do, and the specific plan to succeed.

To make the PSIC formula work — and it really does work — do all of the steps of the formula. Don't leave anything out.

NOTES AND THOUGHTS

NOTES AND THOUGHTS

CHAPTER 2

ACTION ONE —
PLANNING YOUR FORTUNE

The line between planning and dreaming is fine but real. Planning is a dream with the addition of action.

Conrad Hilton, founder of probably the greatest hotel empire in the world, did a lot of dreaming in his younger years, but he didn't stop with a mere dream. He added that all-important extra ingredient — action.

In his autobiography, Mr. Hilton entitled his first chapter "You've Got to Dream," and states:

> Why, when I saw my first photograph of the recently built "new" Waldorf in 1931, read of such luxuries as a private railroad siding in the basement, a private hospital for guests, a golden rivet in her innards where her construction had started, six kitchens, two hundred cooks, five hundred waiters, one hundred dishwashers, not to mention two thousand rooms, I was beating my way around Texas half hidden under a ten-gallon hat, existing on a voluntary loan from a bellboy. My laundry was in hock and a gun-toting constable was trying to find places to hang up the court judgments against me.
>
> It was presumptious, an outrageous time to dream. Still I cut out that picture of the Waldorf and wrote across it, "The Greatest of Them All." As soon as I had won back a desk of my own I slipped the dog-eared clipping under the glass top. From then on it was always in front of me.
>
> Fifteen years later, in October, 1949, "The Greatest of Them All" became a Hilton Hotel.
>
> It had taken a lot of work, four years of delicate negotiation and even before that, careful planning. It had taken a lot of prayer. During the final crucial days I had attended church at six-thirty each morning. No matter how late we

worked into the night, I started the day on my knees. (*Be My Guest* [Englewood Cliffs, N.J.: Prentice-Hall, Inc., 1957], p.18.)

DREAM BIG!

Conrad Hilton started with only a dream — no money — just a big, big dream. But he did what most people are not willing to do. He added action, and turned his imagination into a plan. He gave the plan details, scheduled the details, and made alternate plans in case the first plan failed. Most importantly, he put his plan into action and made it come true.

In Chapter 11 of the same book, he asks, "How Big Can You Dream?" If you don't dream big, you certainly won't achieve much. It is against the basic laws that govern man. Unless you can visualize something, you cannot attain it.

Amazing as it sounds, the great majority of people in the United States don't spend even an hour a week, pencil or pen in hand, planning the strategy for their financial future. Someone once said, "Most people are so busy earning a living, they never make any money." And it's true! Most don't take the time to lift their heads from a mundane, routine life to do more than *dream* of financial security and independence.

They delude themselves into thinking they are happy, that their future is secure because they have a secure, salaried job.

That is not security. Their only security is two weeks' notice and, if they are lucky, some severance pay.

PERSISTENT PLANNING

Action one then in the PSIC formula has to be *persis-*

tent planning. And it has to be done! There is no getting around it. So do it, and do it first.

Can you imagine the builders of the Waldorf Hotel beginning construction without a plan? That would be absurd. They would not only begin with a plan, but the plan would be in the greatest detail and would be written down, even to the last light switch and toilet seat. If detailed plans were not made, the building would be a catastrophe beyond imagination. By the same token, doesn't your financial future deserve, even demand, the same kind of attention and detailed planning?

Of course, a person can't make all his plans in one night, or one week, or even in one month. He must begin where he is. Then he must add to his plans, refine them, and even change them from time to time.

Take the time right now to put your plans on paper. (The following two pages have been left blank for this purpose.)

First, list your goals, both short range and long range, but don't try to be too specific, at least not for now. State your goals in general terms at first. Then break them into more specific actions.

PLANS AND GOALS

PLANS AND GOALS CONT.

FIND YOUR NET WORTH

Now that you have your goals listed, take stock of
your resources. List all your assets. List all your liabilities.
Then subtract your liabilities from your assets, and you
will have an idea of your total net worth.

Now that you know your net worth, use the compound tables in the appendix to start making some hypothetical projections. (See Appendix A.) You will be surprised, even astounded, at what compounding your net
worth can do in a few years.

Check your net worth again. See what kind of liquid
assets (cash or near cash, such as savings, bonds, etc.) you
have and what assets could be quickly and easily turned into cash. Don't overlook what is probably your largest
asset — the equity in your home. (Even in times of high
interest rate that equity can be borrowed against it to
generate just enough cash to launch you into your first
"fantastic bargain.")

PROJECT YOUR FINANCIAL FUTURE

Now, go back, and using the compound tables, make
projections again. At this point you should use only the
liquid assets you have as a base to begin your investments.

Once you have established a financial goal for yourself, you are on your way to achieving it. But you must not
lose sight of that goal. Remember that where one succeeds
because of genius or brilliance, ten succeed because of persistence. Persistence is a rare commodity today. However,
that makes it fortunate for anyone who is persistent. His
persistence will be noticed much more readily.

According to Edward Eggleston, "Persistent people
begin their success where others end in failure." Put your
financial goals in writing and look at them often.

Recalculate on paper the yearly compounding of your initial investment until it takes you to your goal. Do this as frequently as necessary to keep it fresh in your mind.

At least once a month I use a calculator to make all kinds of projections, using different compound rates and different periods of time. In addition, I make out a new balance sheet (assets minus liabilities equals net worth) every two months, in order to measure my progress. This review helps me see where I am making mistakes and gives me an early warning system against lagging behind in my projections. It also motivates me when I review my past successes and helps me dream bigger dreams.

Way back in April 1970, an article "Little Cash Needed on Road to Wealth" in the *Denver Post* quoted Marvin Naiman, then president of the Sherman Agency, "Average people, people able to raise $5,000 to $10,000 cash, have it within their power to become millionaires in real estate within twenty years." Naiman was counseling people with absolutely zero money who he was sure would be rich in a few years. In his view, "Imagination is the essential ingredient — imagination and a little bit of daydreaming."

This is even more true today. People without imagination allow themselves to feel stymied by talk of recession, high interest rates, and tight money. When, in fact, because so many are afraid to venture, opportunities are actually more plentiful.

Dreams put into action through planning are essential to the accumulation of wealth, regardless of changing economic factors.

ONASSIS

Probably my favorite biography is *Onassis,* the story of Aristotle Socrates Onassis, written by Willi Frischauer [New York: Meredith Press, 1968]. The author gives the reader insights into the dreams, desires, and motivations of Aristotle Onassis in his climb to financial success.

Aristotle Onassis was a dreamer, a planner, and probably more than anything, a very persistent person. Mr. Firschauer states:

> More than anything else, Aristotle Onassis wanted to own and run ships; and from the dream and the idea it was only a short step to the intention and the plan. To persuade himself that his plan was sound, he went in for what he called "a little mental gymnastics."
>
> In his mind's eye he visualized a ship with a capacity of half a million cubic feet of grain, which might have cost one million dollars to build in 1919 or 1920. [p. 56.]

Keep in mind that this was before Onassis had even bought his first ship, but he could visualize it in his mind, had done some dreaming, and later set a definite plan of action to acquire such a ship.

At the age of seventeen, without a passport, Onassis arrived in Buenos Aires and lied about his age in order to get a job (for the British United River Plate Telephone Company at twenty-five cents an hour). In his spare time, Ari planned and thought about the feasibility of importing tobacco from Greece to Argentina. He envisioned a market there because Argentina was importing tobaccos primarily from Brazil and Cuba, with only a small percentage of Oriental brands.

PERSISTENCE AND PLANNING

After receiving tobacco samples from his father in Greece, he contacted each of the tobacco companies in

Buenos Aires and was turned down by each in turn. The plans he set into motion after that failure were those that only one person in forty million would have tried. That very kind of planning and persistence made Aristotle Socrates Onassis what he was.

Choosing the firm that seemed to offer the best chance of a sale, he made it his business to track down the managing director, a Senor Juan Gaona, who became the young tobacco salesman's principal target. Early mornings he posted himself at the entrance of the senor's office, standing there without saying a word, looking at Senor Gaona when he arrived and, incidently, looking rather sorry for himself.

On alternate days he transferred his lonely vigil to the important man's home, taking up his position at the door. Wherever the hapless Senor Gaona went, Aristotle Onassis was waiting for him, a sad and silent youngster. After a fortnight of this exercise, Senor Gaona would not have been human had he not begun to wonder what it was about. If it was a battle of perseverance between two unlikely protagonists, Aristotle Onassis emerged as the clear winner. His strange sales campaign was about to enter the third week when Senor Gaona could no longer restrain his curiosity and confronted his silent pursuer.

"Who are you?" he asked in a tone of mixed sympathy and exasperation. "What are you doing here? What do you want?"

"I am trying to sell tobacco," was the simple answer. Aristotle complained that he had not been given a fair chance; the tobacco he had to offer was of excellent quality. Senor Gaona was amused. "You ought to go to my purchasing department," he told Onassis.

This was all the unorthodox tobacco salesman wanted to hear. It was one thing to call on a buyer off his own bat but an entirely different matter to be in a position to say that he had been sent by the managing director. [p. 48.]

Onassis presented his wares the next morning and secured a $10,000 order, from which he made a commission of $500. This must have seemed a fortune to him, compared to the twenty-five cents an hour he was making at the telephone company.

A short time later he received an order that netted him $2,500 in commission. This was only the beginning in his rise to the top. He had understood and used the powerful ingredient of persistent planning.

NOTES AND THOUGHTS

Notes And Thoughts

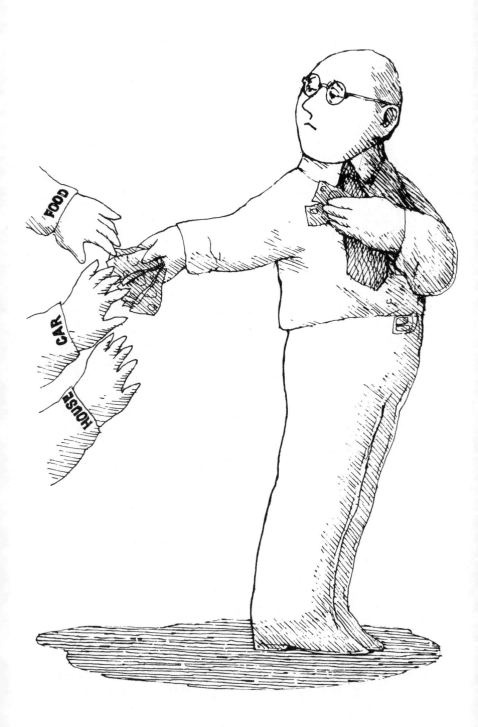

CHAPTER 3

ACTION TWO —
SAVING THE MAGIC
10 PERCENT

To belong to that exclusive group of millionaires — the one out of a thousand — you must begin by following the 10 percent rule. Any increase in the 10 percent rule speeds you on the way to making your fortune.

William Nickerson in his book *How I Turned $1,000 into Three Million in Real Estate — in My Spare Time* [New York: Simon and Schuster, 1969] states, "Starting with average funds can speed the way to financial success. The hardest task on the road to a million dollars is saving a nest egg." (p. 23.) As soon as the typical American has a small amount of money saved, he is tempted to spend it on depreciating assets such as a car, a camper, boat, trailer, or an exotic vacation.

Most people spend their entire lives saving just enough to buy something to keep up with their neighbors. They never have enough left over to make any meaningful investments.

PAY YOURSELF FIRST

The 10 percent rule is a simple one, but a difficult one for some to follow. You must save a minimum of 10 percent of your gross earnings. The second part of the rule is that you never, never, never, never spend that savings. Your capital is your savings, and your capital must never be disturbed. Let me repeat, NEVER spend your savings! Now, spending is different than investing.

Many claim they cannot save money. They say it is impossible on their income and constantly rising expenses, that when the end of the month rolls around there is nothing left. The solution is simple: Pay yourself first. If you do this, faithfully, religiously, and without ever missing a single paycheck, you will find that this 10 percent of every dollar you earn will (with careful and astute investing) mushroom into a sum that will far exceed your total lifetime earnings.

The Bible talks about the importance of the 10 percent rule in a different way. Early Christians were encouraged and even commanded to pay one-tenth of their annual increase to the Church. In modern times, The Church of Jesus Christ of Latter-day Saints (the Mormons) uses this ancient biblical doctrine of the tithe.

The amazing thing about the Mormons and tithing is that, notwithstanding the large donations made by many of the Mormons, it is estimated that there are more than three thousand millionaires in that small church. From first-hand observation, many of the other members enjoy a much higher standard of living than any other group of people in the world; and all of this after they have given 10 percent of their gross earnings to their church.

MORMONS CAN! CAN YOU?

The Mormons claim that by giving 10 percent to their church they are better able to plan ahead and use wisely the balance of their money. Even poor widows and retired people on dwindling incomes caused by inflation seem to be able to make this contribution without crimping their life style. This contradicts the belief that expenses always rise to meet the income.

Mormons stress that payment of tithing should be done first, before bills and expenses. Likewise, as stated before, in your financial program you should always PAY YOURSELF FIRST.

If you still don't think you can achieve the 10 percent savings goal, try this line of reasoning: What if you worked for a troubled corporation that was going downhill financially, at least temporarily, in an industry that was faced with a recession? Your boss tells you that he has been ordered to cut your department by 10 percent. Rather than firing 10 percent of the employees, he is giving you all the choice of taking a 10 percent pay cut until the corporation gets on its feet again. What will your choice be? Remember that there is a recession in progress and unemployment is soaring. You know that it would be difficult to find another job.

It is a good bet that you would conclude that you could somehow get by on 10 percent less income. No, it won't be easy, but with a little effort it can be done. It means cutting out things you don't really have to have. (By the way, this became cold reality for some 1,700 top executives of the Chrysler Corporation as that automobile manufacturing giant fought for its economic survival. The company not only sought aid from the federal government, it also slashed salaries by 10 percent in an attempt to reduce a crippling deficit.)

ADD TO THE 10 PERCENT

Once you have control of your income and are saving 10 percent, the next time you get any kind of an increase either through a salary raise or through a decrease in deductions, put all the extra you receive into your savings program. This will speed up the achievement of the million-dollar goal.

If you look back at the compounding of a penny on pages 1-3, you will see that in the early stages of compounding with such a low sum the total accumulation of money is very small. If you were to take out even a small amount in those first few steps (for example, take out twenty-five cents on the sixth day), the results are devastating. However, if you take out large amounts in the last few steps, you could spend literally millions a year without even denting your total assets. (What would be the effect if from the thirty-third day on, you spent $5,000,000 each day?) Likewise, if you add money in the beginning stages, that addition has a tremendous effect, especially toward the end. Just for fun, try starting with $10,000 versus one penny on a thirty-five-step basis.

Retirement: Tragedy Or Capital Investments

The importance of saving to get started on your way to a million should be the most glaringly simple deduction to anyone who has common sense and reasoning power. But obviously it is not that apparent to most men and women.

I believe it was Earl Nightingale who quoted some tragic statistics regarding a hundred average people at the age of retirement. In this sample, pre-suppose that all had started work at the age of twenty-five; all received encouragement from parents, teachers, and friends; and all shared the dream of success and wealth. After forty years of hard work, only one of the hundred would be rich, truly rich; four would be financially independent; five would still be working; thirty-six would be dead; and fifty-four would be broke. This is a sad situation in a country with so much opportunity and so much wealth.

The reason for these tragic statistics is that people don't save, they don't begin at the beginning. They don't even acquire what is known as *capital*. Virtually every wealthy individual has begun his fortune by first saving until he had enough capital to begin investing.

JOHN D.

The grandaddy of super wealth, John Davidson Rockefeller, born in Richford, New York, 8 July 1839, realized and utilized this principle.

At sixteen years of age, John D., with probably America's most determined ambition to build up a large and useful business — and therefore successful — set out for a job. The firm of Hewitt and Tuttle hired him for $50 for services from September 26 to December 31 inclusive — about $3.74 a week. The firm handled grain, produce, coal — in fact, every commodity that passed through Cleveland going east or west. It shipped by rail, canal and lake and offered an ideal training ground for the young man. He studied every phase of the business. He checked in every detail every bill before it was paid. Argued with dealers for better prices. Knew just exactly where the business stood every night.

And Hewitt and Tuttle knew they had a find in young Rockefeller. Nothing distracted him from the affairs of the business. No boisterous fun for him. No cigarettes; no cards; no pool; no girls. Just plenty of work and plenty of Sunday School. His soft voice, and his quiet clothes and his devotion to the Baptist Church early earned for him the nickname of Deacon.

He stayed on this first job two and a half years at a meager salary although he had been rapidly advanced in responsibility. He finally asked for a salary of $800 a year. The employers held out with an offer of $700. During this deadlock, a chance came to John D. to join in a partnership and he was lost from the firm of Hewitt and Tuttle.

This partnership was formed before John D. was nineteen, with a young Englishman named Clark who had $2,000 to put into a commission business and who wanted two partners with equal capital. Even on a low income, the youthful Rockefeller had managed to put aside $1,000. He was to receive another $1,000 from his father when he turned twenty-one. He asked his strict parent if he might not have his $1,000 then so that he might not lose his opportunity. The father consented but only on the condition that he pay him 10 percent interest per year until he was twenty-one.

Rockefeller is not an isolated incident. There is example after example of people on meager salaries saving faithfully and religiously until they have a nest egg large enough to make that initial investment. Each one realized, as everyone must who is going to make substantial sums, that capital must work for you as hard or harder than you work, in order to reach the million-dollar goal. Cornelius Vanderbilt is one of many who had saved $1,000 by the time he was eighteen years old and $9,000 by the time he was twenty-three. Those savings came from meager amounts of income.

Whether your income is $5,000 or $50,000 a year, it is still possible to apply the 10 percent rule and become part of a distinguished group, the one out of a thousand who reaches the million-dollar mark.

Remember that for every $10,000 you can save, given eighteen years and 30 percent annual compound rate of return (which is not difficult to achieve), you will have $1,124,000.00.

Notes And Thoughts

CHAPTER 4

ACTION THREE — HIGH RATES OF RETURN

A famous and wealthy man said, "Ninety percent of all millionaires become so through owning real estate. More money has been made in real estate than in all industrial investments combined. The wise young man or wage earner of today invests his money in real estate." That statement is truer today than it was when Andrew Carnegie made it.

There is a multitude of different types and sizes of investments. And there are even more people representing these investments, vying for our investment dollar. But of the hundreds of available investments I know of none that offers as many basic advantages as real estate. These advantages put the odds overwhelmingly in your favor for succeeding in the pursuit of wealth. The four basic advantages of real estate, which we talk about in detail later, are (1) cash flow that is usually higher than in other investments; (2) equity buildup that can dramatically increase the overall return; (3) inflation, both natural and forced; and (4) a tax shelter that very few other investments offer.

THE ODDS ARE HEAVILY IN YOUR FAVOR

William Nickerson thinks real estate is the best investment because it is so easy to use other people's money. As he puts it:

> Most forms of investment pay only the paltry leavings
> after others deduct their expenses and fair compensation

for using your money. You lend your savings to banks and insurance companies, and they capitalize on your money for their profit.

Investment in business and income property puts you on the real money-making side of the capital fence and pays you for courage and imagination. You profit not only from your own savings but also from the savings of the timid, the uninformed, and the satiated who already possess all the money they want.

Every venture presents an element of risk, but with rent-producing income property you take negligible risks and your chances for success are 1,600 times better, for example, than your chances if you start in business. With each, however, you follow the freeway that leads to wealth by harnessing the secret force of capitalism — which is the pyramiding power of borrowed money. Regardless of how wisely you invest, you can't go far on your own money. Your greatest expansion is assured by making maximum use of the other fellow's money.

The road to riches is paved with borrowed money. Big-time real estate operators buy properties worth millions without putting in a penny of their own. Multimillion-dollar deals are made by borrowing the utmost from mortgages and the balance on personal and collateral notes. (*How I Turned $1,000 into Three Million,* p. 13.)

Nickerson gets his figures — the odds of 1,600 to one — from the Department of Commerce which states that four out of five new businesses fail within eight years. Additionally, 50 percent go out of business within two years. The overall odds are four to one that a new business will not make it. He contrasts those four-to-one odds against real estate investments, where only one out of four hundred properties is foreclosed, establishing the odds of four hundred to one in favor of you succeeding. By combining these two sets of statistics, he comes up with 1,600 to one odds for success in income property.

In addition to the four basic advantages of real estate,

two others reduce the risk of loss. First, housing is a basic necessity. Most investments, such as stocks, bonds, motels, hotels, resorts and miscellaneous businesses, do not have this advantage. Those investments normally are made when basic necessities have already been taken care of. Virtually every person in this country wants to upgrade his housing by moving into something nicer, thus creating a constant demand and a demand that only moves upward.

This demand is increased by the birth rate and by new families formed through marriage. In some areas there is the added benefit of the movement of people from one state to another. The Western states and the Sun Belt in the last fifteen to twenty years have benefitted most by such migration. Current statistics show this pattern continuing with the these states having the greatest percentage increases.

With this advantage it is difficult to fail by ownership of income properties. Even without the advantage of migration of people into your state or community the odds of success are heavily in your favor.

The second big advantage is the control one has with income properties. With stocks, you not only do not control the market and the fluctuation of the market, you do not even control the corporation in which you have invested. If the president of the corporation makes an unwise decision, you have no recourse (assuming you do not have controlling interest). In the ownership of income-producing properties, you do not have absolute control over the market; however, through the management of your property over which you have 100 percent control, you can influence the market and better your position if necessary.

Your primary concern in projecting the growth of your net worth should be the return on equity (the return you get from investing whatever dollars you have). Specifically, all you care about is the overall return you receive when you add up the four advantages of real estate: (1) cash flow, (2) equity buildup, (3) inflation, and (4) tax shelter or tax advantages.

Cash Flow — To Reinvest Not Spend

First of all, *cash flow* in real estate investing can be very high and has consistently been higher than other types of investments. Cash flow can make a tremendous difference in the rate of growth in acquiring a fortune.

It is simple to calculate the cash flow figure. You need only two answers: (1) How much out-of-pocket money did you put into the investment? (2) How much money did you get out of the deal (put in your pocket) in one year? If you put in $5,000 cash and took out $1,000 in one year, your cash flow was 20 percent ($1,000 \div 5,000 = 20$ percent). Cash flow is the first thing you should look for in evaluating a real estate investment. Remember, if you get an extremely high cash flow, you can take that cash and reinvest it in another similar investment. This gives the compounding effect to your money and can work miracles in a short period of time.

In older real estate, cash flow should be at an absolute minimum of 10 percent, after all contingencies, vacancies, and other costs, both expected and unexpected. Whereas 10 percent is the minimum, many times a much higher rate of return on a cash flow basis can be achieved. I have had real estate investments where the cash flow exceeded 100 percent; in two cases the cash flow actually exceeded 200 percent per year. With a little calculating, you see how quickly you can rise in the early years if you find this type of investment. It is important to look for the proper investment vehicle. Your hours of searching for the super bargains in real estate will be amply rewarded. I have never known anyone who put in the hours looking for bargains that didn't find at least a few good deals.

EQUITY BUILDUP —
ADDS TO YOUR WEALTH MONTHLY

The second advantage to real estate investments is the *equity buildup* or the amount of principal payment made to reduce the mortgage loan. This payment, of course, is made from the gross income (rental income from tenants of your buildings). When the equity buildup is calculated as a rate of return on the initial equity you put into an investment, the return can vary widely depending on the length of time of the mortgage, the interest rate, and the amount of the beginning equity (down payment). Typically, the equity buildup figure should be in the neighborhood of 3 percent to 5 percent for an average twenty-five year loan with an interest rate of 10 percent to 14 percent and a 10 percent to 20 percent down payment.

Let's say you find an apartment building that looks like an attractive investment but the cash flow is only 10.5 percent. In checking further you find that the mortgage loan on the building will be completely amortized in only thirteen and-a-half years and you need only a 10 percent down payment. When you put a pencil to it, you would find that it very well could be a super bargain. That is, even though the cash flow is not particularly high at 10.5 percent, if you are paying 9 percent interest on the mortgage, the equity buildup would be in the neighborhood of 40 percent per year. This added to the 10.5 percent cash flow gives an overall return of better than 50 percent a year. And that is before we take into account the next two factors of inflation and tax advantage or tax shelter.

Inflation — The Key That Will Double Your Net Worth Yearly

Inflation or appreciation is the third ingredient that adds to the overall return of investments in real estate. There are several causes of inflation. Without trying to debate who and what causes inflation, there is no question that continued deficit spending by our government is a prime factor. But whatever the causes, there can be benefits to inflation if the investor realizes proper and wise use of leverage. Let me illustrate with a simplified example. Say you bought a $100,000 piece of income-producing property. Assume you paid $10,000 down, with the $90,000 balance owing to either the seller or through a mortgage to a bank, and possibly a second mortgage. You would begin making monthly payments on the mortgages. These would be made from the rents you collect each month.

Even if you didn't have any cash left over at the end of each month (cash flow), what would be your situation, assuming that this particular piece of real estate inflated for whatever reason by 10 percent in one year? First of all, what would be the worth of that building at the end of the year? With simple mathematics, it is obvious the building would be worth $110,000. By subtracting the $90,000 mortgage or slightly less because of payments toward the principal (equity buildup), the balance would equal your new net equity in the building. What has this 10 percent inflation done to your return (assuming you were to sell the building)? The magic of leverage can be seen in this simple example. Even though the building only grew in worth by 10 percent, your return was an astounding 100 percent. (See Chapters 6 and 7 for detailed explanations and examples of leverage.)

It is not likely that real estate by itself will appreciate

or inflate at a 10 percent rate per year. Depending on the area of the country and locations within particular towns, the rate of so-called natural inflation has been anywhere from 1.5 percent to 4.5 percent per year.

There is another kind of inflation, however, that really should not be called inflation, but that's what I call it. What I call *forced inflation* could probably more properly be called *appreciation through improvements.* Forced inflation can be used over and over again in virtually every city and also in concert with natural inflation. What forced inflation does is simple: it creates higher worth of a particular real estate investment (income property), brought about by improvements to that property. Using the former example of a $100,000 building that improved in value by 10 percent in one year, if this building were to actually inflate in value only 2 percent in a given year and your program called for an increase in net equities of 100 percent, you would have to do something to bring about an increase. And you could! That would be to bring about forced inflation or improvements to the property to increase the worth of the investments to the desired level. (See Chapter 12 on improvement to sell or manage to keep.)

Even if one plans on only the natural inflation and assuming that inflation is a 2 percent factor on the $100,000 property, this is still a 20 percent rate of return on the original $10,000 investment (2 percent on $100,000 equals $2,000 annually; this $2,000 would be a 20 percent return on the original $10,000 down payment). The extra rate of return derived from inflation when added to cash flow and equity buildup makes our real estate investment an unusual and attractive way to invest money. Of course, if we stop after one or two investments in real estate, we don't get the compounding effect. (See Chapter 5 on compounding or reinvesting our return.)

TAX SHELTER: SHORT CUT TO WEALTH

The fourth fact that makes real estate investments so attractive and adds immensely to the overall return is *tax shelter* or tax advantage. Let me ask a simple question: How long would it take a person to make a million starting with $10,000 and investing the money at a consistent 25 percent compounded rate of return? I will even help you out by providing a chart on page 43. By using the chart, the obvious answer would be twenty-one years. Right? Wrong! Why? Because of that government agency we are all familiar with — the IRS. Yes, Uncle Sam takes a big part, an ever-growing part of our income.

To answer the above question we must know two additional facts: What income tax bracket is the person in and what type of investments is he making? Let's make two assumptions: This person is in a 50 percent tax bracket and he is making general types of investments in stocks and bonds and various small businesses. OK. And now the question again: How long would it take this person to make $1 million with $10,000 compounding at 25 percent? If you want to take the time to figure it, the simple way is just to compound $10,000 at an annual rate of 12.5 percent. The answer could be stated this way: If the person were thirty years of age when he began this program, made the investments we mentioned and paid average taxes, he would be seventy years old by the time he reached the million-dollar mark. It would have taken him forty years.

Now, compare the man who made real estate investments, paid no tax because of the preferential treatment he can take advantage of (see Chapter 13 on taxes), and he reaches the goal by age fifty-one, or in twenty-one years. Through the wise use of current tax laws, one person was

EXAMPLE OF COMPOUNDING
($10,000 at 25 percent for 21 years)

Years

0	$ 10,000
1	12,500
2	15,600
3	19,531
4	24,414
5	30,500
6	38,125
7	47,656
8	59,500
9	74,375
10	92,969
11	116,125
12	145,156
13	181,445
14	226,250
15	282,812
16	353,515
17	441,259
18	551,562
19	689,453
20	861,250
21	$1,076,562

Note: Several of the above figures have
been rounded off for ease in figuring.

able to enjoy his fortune nineteen years longer than the one who did not take advantage of the same tax laws.

This fourth advantage of real estate investing adds anywhere from 2 percent to 3 percent advantage on the low side on the overall return on equity up to 40 percent or 50 percent on the high side, all dependent on the person's tax bracket and the particular real estate investment.

In addition to the advantages mentioned, income property investments can shelter income from other sources such as salary, commissions, fees, other capital gains. This too will be talked about in Chapter 13.

When the four basic types of return in a real estate investment are tabulated, the total potential seems almost unbelievable and unachievable. Whereas it is difficult to find real estate investments that have the high side of the range in all four categories (225 percent), it is not impossible and can be done regularly if enough effort is put into the task. Below is a tabulation of the four ingredients to real estate investment:

Type of Return	Annual Percentage Rate of Return on Beginning Equity
Cash Flow	10% to 25%
Equity Buildup	3% to 45%
Inflation	10% to 105%
Tax Advantage	2% to 50%
	25% to 225%

To many people, the range of 25 percent on the low to 225 percent on the high side seems too optimistic for the total return on equity. Believe me, these are not pie-in-the-sky figures. These are down-to-earth figures and are achievable on a consistent basis. Where you end up on that scale is up to you and depends on how much effort you put into locating the right investment, bargaining for the price and terms, buying the property, making necessary changes, and disposing of the property in a way that is advantageous from a tax standpoint.

Some might question whether it is worth the effort to try to reach the higher end of the scale — 225 percent. If that is your attitude, I suggest you sit down with a calculator and find the results on any size investment with a 225 percent compound rate of return. I think you will find enough motivation from your calculations to answer whether it is worth the effort to you.

In my program I have not yet reached the high end of the scale. I have come close with an overall return of a little better than 160 percent. On individual investments I have reached the 225 percent mark. I know others who have hit the high mark consistently, so I know it can be done. If you are the ambitious and persistent type, you might well be one who can do it. Even if you only muster out at a 25 percent or 30 percent return and stick with it, your million-dollar daydream will become a reality.

NOTES AND THOUGHTS

NOTES AND THOUGHTS

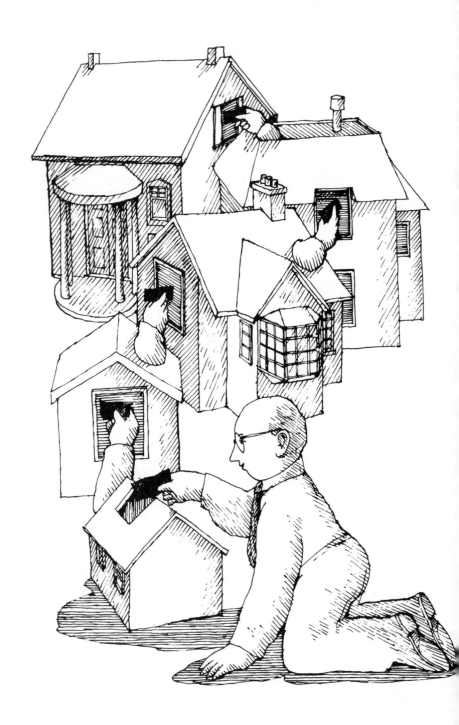

CHAPTER 5

ACTION FOUR —
REINVEST TO COMPOUND

The story is told about a visitor to an older New England town of great affluence. The town was conservative, with most of its residents middle-aged, retired gentlemen and their wives. While walking one day with one of the town's well-known residents, the visitor noticed a stately old gentleman walking down the street. As he walked, it seemed that everyone went out of the way to avoid him, even if it meant going to the other side of the street. Puzzled, the visitor asked his host who this seemingly undesirable man was and why the people were avoiding him. Whereupon the host stopped abruptly, looked in all directions to make sure he couldn't be heard, leaned over and whispered in the visitor's ear, "He dipped into his capital."

Obviously, these people, men of great means, fully understood the seriousness and potentially dire consequences of spending one's capital. A cardinal rule with wealthy families of the past was, "Never, never, never touch your capital." A rule that you must incorporate and follow to the letter if you expect to attain your million-dollar goal is; never, never, never spend or touch your return on investments in the beginning years of your investment program. And, of course, you must follow the rule of never touching your capital.

Take a minute and turn back to Chapter 1 (page 1 to 3). Look at the example of one penny compounded at 100 percent. Note what a devastating effect could come from

touching the capital or return on that capital in the first
few days. For example, see what happens to the end result
if twelve cents is spent on the fifth day or $5.10 is taken
out on the tenth day. How many days would you lose?
How much money would you lose in the overall investment plan? If we change the days to years, then how much
time or money are we losing by dipping into our capital in
the fifth or tenth year? How does this affect the total in
later years?

If you took the time to figure it out, you saw that the
results were disastrous in the early years. On the other
hand, would it shake your fortune very much to take out a
million dollars after thirty-two, thirty-three, or thirty-four
years? Would it result in much of a change in your overall
net worth? As you can plainly see, the effect would not be
worth mentioning. Isn't this the obvious reason that the
rich and the super rich can afford to be so generous with
their wealth, and it never seems to flicker their financial
light? (Of course, there are also tax advantages to making
these large donations.)

Early in my investment program, I began saving at
least 10 percent of my income, then investing that 10 percent, and reinvesting the income from the investment. It
wasn't until much later that my secretary told me about an
interesting book that expounded the virtues and the
necessity of using these principles to accumulate great
wealth. The book was written by George S. Clason (*The
Richest Man in Babylon* [New York: Hawthorn Books,
Inc., 1955]). In this delightful book a man by the name of
Arkad who is not only very wealthy but known for his
generosity to charities, family, and friends, is asked by his
friends how he became the richest man in all of Babylon
while they were still struggling for their very existence.
They were puzzled because Arkad had been one of their

playmates and they had all attended the same school. They pointed out to Arkad that in neither athletics nor studies did he outshine them. Why had he become so wealthy and they hadn't? Here is Arkad's answer to his contemporaries:

"Being, as you know, the son of a humble merchant, one of a large family, with no hope of an inheritance, and not being endowed, as you have so frankly said, with superior powers or wisdom, I decided that if I was to achieve what I desired, time and study would be required.

"As for time, all men have it in abundance. You, each of you, have let slip by sufficient time to have made yourselves wealthy. Yet, you admit, you have nothing to show except your good families, of which you can be justly proud.

"As for study, did not our wise teacher teach us that learning was of two kinds: the one kind being the things we learned and knew, and the other being in the training that taught us how to find out what we did not know?

"Therefore did I decide to find out how one might accumulate wealth, and when I had found out, to make this my task and do it well. For, is it not wise that we should enjoy while we dwell in the brightness of that sunshine, for sorrows enough shall descend upon us when we depart for the darkness of the world of spirit?

"I found employment as a scribe in the hall of records, and long hours each day I labored upon the clay tablets. Week after week, and month after month, I labored, yet for my earnings I had naught to show. Food and clothing and penance to the gods, and other things of which I could remember not what, absorbed all my earnings. But my determination did not leave me.

"And one day Algamish, the money lender, came to

the house of the city master and ordered a copy of the Ninth Law, and he said to me, 'I must have this in two days, and if the task is done by that time, two coppers will I give to thee.'

"So I labored hard, but the law was long, and when Algamish returned the task was unfinished. He was angry, and had I been his slave, he would have beaten me. But knowing the city master would not permit him to injure me, I was unafraid, so I said to him, 'Algamish, you are a very rich man. Tell me how I may also become rich, and all night I will carve upon the clay, and when the sun rises it shall be completed.'

"He smiled at me and replied, 'You are a forward knave, but we will call it a bargain.'

"All that night I carved, though my back pained and the smell of the wick made my head ache until my eyes could hardly see. But when he returned at sunup, the tablets were complete.

" 'Now,' I said, 'tell me what you promised.'

" 'You have fulfilled your part of our bargain, my son,' he said to me kindly, 'and I am ready to fulfill mine. I will tell you these things you wish to know because I am becoming an old man, and an old tongue loves to wag. And when youth comes to age for advice he receives the wisdom of years. But too often does youth think that age knows only the wisdom of days that are gone, and therefore profits not. But remember this, the sun that shines today is the sun that shone when thy father was born, and will still be shining when thy last grandchild shall pass into the darkness.

" 'The thoughts of youth,' he continued, 'are bright lights that shine forth like the meteors that oft make brilliant the sky, but the wisdom of age is like the fixed stars that shine so unchanged that the sailor may depend upon them to steer his course.

" 'Mark you well my words, for if you do not you will fail to grasp the truth that I will tell you, and you will think that your night's work has been in vain.'

"Then he looked at me shrewdly from under his shaggy brows and said in a low, forceful tone, 'I found the road to wealth when I decided that *a part of all I earned was mine to keep*. And so will you.'

"Then he continued to look at me with a glance that I could feel pierce me but said no more.

" 'Is that all?' I asked.

" 'That was sufficient to change the heart of a sheep herder into the heart of a money lender,' he replied.

" 'But *all* I earn is mine to keep, is it not?' I demanded.

" 'Far from it,' he replied. 'Do you not pay the garment-maker? Do you not pay the sandal-maker? Do you not pay for the things you eat? Can you live in Babylon without spending? What have you to show for your earnings of the past month? What for the past year? Fool! You pay to everyone but yourself. Dullard, you labor for others. As well be a slave and work for what your master gives you to eat and wear. If you did keep for yourself one-tenth of all you earn, how much would you have in ten years?'

"My knowledge of the numbers did not forsake me and I answered, 'As much as I earn in one year.'

" 'You speak but half the truth,' he retorted. 'Every gold piece you save is a slave to work for you. Every copper it earns is its child that also can earn for you. If you would become wealthy, then what you save must earn, and its children must earn, that all may help to give to you the abundance you crave.

" 'You think I cheat you for your long night's work,' he continued, 'but I am paying you a thousand times over if you have the intelligence to grasp the truth I offer you.

" 'A part of all you earn is yours to keep. It should be not less than a tenth no matter how little you earn. It can be as much more as you can afford. Pay yourself first. Do not buy from the clothes-maker and the sandal-maker more than you can pay out of the rest and still have enough for food and charity and penance to the gods.

" 'Wealth, like a tree, grows from a tiny seed. The first copper you save is the seed from which your tree of wealth shall grow. The sooner you plant that seed the sooner shall the tree grow. And the more faithfully you nourish and water that tree with consistent savings, the sooner may you bask in contentment beneath its shade.'

"So saying, he took his tablets and went away.

"I thought much about what he had said to me, and it seemed reasonable. So I decided that I would try it. Each time I was paid I took one from each ten pieces of copper and hid it away. And strange as it may seem, I was no shorter of funds than before. I noticed little difference as I managed to get along without it. But often I was tempted, as my hoard began to grow, to spend it for some of the good things the merchants displayed, brought by camels and ships from the land of the Phoenicians. But I wisely refrained.

"A twelfth month after Algamish had gone he again returned and said to me, 'Son, have you paid to yourself not less than one-tenth of all you have earned in the past year?'

"I answered proudly, 'Yes, master, I have.'

" 'That is good,' he answered beaming upon me, 'and what have you done with it?'

" 'I have given it to Azmur, the brickmaker, who told me he was traveling over the far seas and in Tyre he would buy for me the rare jewels of the Phoenicians. When he returns we shall sell these at high prices and divide the earnings.'

" 'Every fool must learn,' he growled, 'but why trust the knowledge of a brickmaker about jewels? Would you go the breadmaker to inquire about the stars? No, by my tunic, you would go to the astrologer, if you had power to think. Your savings are gone, youth, you have jerked your wealth-tree up by the roots. But plant another. Try again. And next time if you would have advice about jewels, go to the jewel merchant. If you would know the truth about sheep, go the herdsman. Advice is one thing that is freely given away, but watch that you take only what is worth having. He who takes advice about his savings from one who is inexperienced in such matters, shall pay with his savings for proving the falsity of their opinions.' Saying this, he went away.

"And it was as he said. For the Phoenicians are scoundrels and sold to Azmur worthless bits of glass that looked like gems. But as Algamish had bid me, I again saved each tenth copper, for I now had formed the habit and it was no longer difficult.

"Again, twelve months later, Algamish came to the room of the scribes and addressed me. 'What progress have you made since last I saw you?'

" 'I have paid myself faithfully,' I replied, 'and my savings I have entrusted to Agger the shieldmaker, to buy bronze, and each fourth month he does pay me the rental.'

" 'That is good. And what do you do with the rental?'

" 'I do have a great feast with honey and fine wine and spiced cake. Also I have bought me a scarlet tunic. And some day I shall buy me a young ass upon which to ride.'

"To which Algamish laughed, 'You do eat the

children of your savings. Then how do you expect them to work for you? And how can they have children that will also work for you? First get thee an army of golden slaves and then many a rich banquet may you enjoy without regret.' So saying he again went away.

"Nor did I again see him for two years, when he once more returned and his face was full of deep lines and his eyes drooped, for he was becoming a very old man. And he said to me, 'Arkad, hast thou yet achieved the wealth thou dreamed of?'

"And I answered, 'Not yet all that I desire, but some I have and it earns more, and its earnings earn more.'

" 'And do you still take the advice of brickmakers?'

" 'About brickmaking they give good advice,' I retorted.

" 'Arkad,' he continued, 'you have learned your lessons well. You first learned to live upon less than you could earn. Next you learned to seek advice from those who were competent through their own experiences to give it. And, lastly, you have learned to make gold work for you.' " (*The Richest Man in Babylon,* pp. 23-29.)

After you have taken great efforts to plan, save and invest, remember the words of Algamish to Arkad when he found that Arkad was having a great feast each time he received a return on his investment, "You do eat the children of your savings. Then how do you expect them to work for you? And how can they have children that will also work for you? First, get thee an army of golden slaves and then many a rich banquet may you enjoy without regret."

Within this story of Arkad lie all of the basics in general form of the PSIC formula. All that needs to be added to this story are the specifics of how to invest and what to invest in to bring the highest possible return on your investment. Then it will be up to you to achieve your million-dollar goal in the shortest possible time. The following chapters give you the specific instructions.

Notes And Thoughts

Notes And Thoughts

NOTES AND THOUGHTS

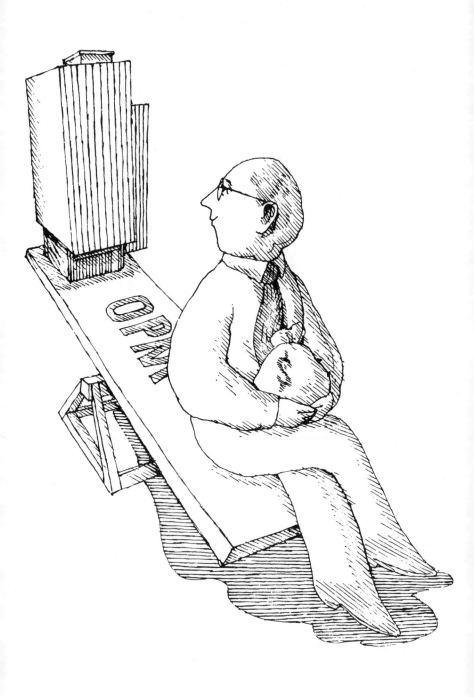

CHAPTER 6

LEVERAGE — MOST POWERFUL TOOL IN YOUR BAG

Archimedes, the Greek mathematician and physicist, calculated the law of the lever. He is reported to have said that if he had a lever long enough and a place to stand, he alone could lift the world.

In real estate the same principle applies: If you have a long enough lever, you can lift or buy properties that are so large that you heretofore have not even dreamed of such purchases. The OPM formula — Other People's Money — is the formula for using leverage. In real estate, leverage is implemented by using borrowed money. You use leverage when you buy, for example, a $100,000 piece of property with $10,000 of your own money. The financing or $90,000 is in effect the lever. Your $10,000 is the weight that pushes the lever down in order to lift the $100,000 piece of property. Leverage is the most powerful tool in your entire investor's bag of tools. If wisely used, this tool can and will, regardless of your starting position, make you as rich as you have the energy to follow through and continue to purchase properties.

HENRY FORD DIDN'T INVEST A PENNY OF HIS OWN MONEY

Leverage can also be used in a myriad of business and other ventures, in addition to real estate. Henry Ford mastered the use of leverage. In fact, in building his auto empire, Henry Ford did not invest even one cent of his own money. His contribution was "sweat equity" so named by Arthur Cohen who, starting with $25,000 in 1954, has done in real estate what, to most, seems utterly impossible. Mr. Cohen now controls in excess of $1.7 billion of U.S. real estate. Quoting from the book *The Young Millionaires* by Laurence A. Armour, "The basic 'play' in real estate is to make money with other people's money — e.g., mortgage money." ([Chicago: Playboy Press, 1973], p. 186.) (More of Mr. Cohen in Chapter 7.) As a matter of fact, a large percentage of businesses today incorporate leverage as a basis of increasing their growth rate.

CASH VERSUS LEVERAGE

The biggest advantage of leverage in real estate lies in entry into the market. If you did not have a big nest egg or a great amount of assets, you would have a difficult time using the 10 percent leverage in starting your own business or even in buying a corporation or small business. By comparison, someone just starting out in real estate can use 90 percent leverage, and more, particularly on income property. For example, if you were planning to start your own business and had saved $20,000, you would have a very difficult time borrowing more than $20,000 additional from a bank to leverage your business into an increased growth rate. True, friends with money might possibly loan you additional funds to increase your leverage.

But compare this situation to an investment in real estate. Even if you have no prior experience in buying properties and have scrimped and saved $10,000, without much difficulty you could find and purchase an income property valued at $80,000 to $100,000. If you looked hard and ended up with a property valued at $100,000, your leverage factor would be 90 percent. That means 90 percent of your investment would come from other people's money (probably in first and second mortgage money). In the previous example of starting your own business, your leverage factor would be 50 percent.

You may say at this point, so what? Why such a fuss over the amount of leverage? Couldn't borrowing all that money hurt me? And even if it doesn't hurt me, how can it help me?

Well, let's answer these questions with an example. Assume that you have $20,000 and you have decided that your odds are greater in real estate. You're to the point of comparing two pieces of real estate. They are both income-producing properties, but their sizes are different. One is $200,000 in multiple units. The other is a $20,000 single unit. The $200,000 property can be purchased on a favorable leverage basis — $20,000 down and first and second mortgage money (the seller has agreed to carry a second mortgage). On the other hand, the small unit is to be sold for $20,000 cash.

Before the hypothetical purchase, let's make another assumption. Assume that inflation continues as in the past. After purchasing the property we would get lucky and have a big jump in inflation. For example, if we had a 10 percent inflation in buildings, one year later the purchase you made would be worth 10 percent more than you paid for it. For the time being, completely forget about the cash flow, equity buildup, and tax benefits you would inevitably receive from such a purchase. Without these extra benefits, from inflation alone (assuming you sold the building for the new increased value), what would be the rate of return on your investment?

First, had you chosen the smaller investment, the 10 percent return or increase on the building would bring the value to $22,000, making a profit of $2,000. However, had you chosen the highly leveraged investment, the value at the end of the year would have increased to $220,000. Since your investment would have been $20,000, with a return of $20,000 your rate of return would be an amazing 100 percent. Remember, that was with an increase of only 10 percent. You would have actually made 100 percent on a 10 percent increase in the value of the building! In this simplified example (I have had many deals that have been just this simple) you easily can see why leverage is the most powerful tool in real estate investments because even if it took two years, or even five, to increase in value by 10 percent, you have made a tremendous return on the appreciation of the property. (Start adding in the other three factors — cash flow, equity buildup, and the tax advantage — and your rate of return becomes phenomenal.)

What if inflation stops? First, don't stand on one foot until that happens. Second, in periods when it slows down, you could always implement that extra ingredient — forced inflation or planned property improvement — and increase the value, regardless of what inflation has or has not done to it. (See Chapter 12.)

Even A Bad Buy Can Make Money

One of my earlier investments, and the smallest one I have ever made in real estate, looked at one time as though it were a disaster. I bought a single family unit in a poor location of Salt Lake City; in fact, the exact location was 542 South 10th West in a mixed neighborhood of dubious reputation. I had bought the home in a hurry, believing it to be a real steal because of the price and terms. The owner was asking around $9,000 for the home; I made a quick offer of $7,500 with only $700 down and the balance on a uniform real-estate contract at 7 percent interest at $80 a month. From a leverage standpoint, it was a very good investment. Much to my surprise and delight — at the time — the owner accepted my offer. On closer inspection, I found the property was structurally unsound. The house had been built many years before, on the dirt without a foundation. The dirt settled and moved, and the corners of the house had sagged until there wasn't a level floor in the house.

Undaunted, I forged ahead with planned renovations. I brought in a crew of young men, fifteen- and sixteen-year-olds, on a hot summer morning. I don't remember how many, but we had quite a crew. Some were painting, some cleaning, some sweeping, some cutting the grass, trimming hedges, or laying carpet. There I was orchestrating the activities in an attempt to avert a disaster. Well, somehow we managed to get the job done. When the bills rolled in, I had spent another $1,300 on renovations. That didn't bother me, because with its new paint, carpets, and drapes the house looked neat and tidy. I quickly rented it for $155 a month, giving after all expenses a $50 spendable income. Based on the rent I was receiving, I estimated the worth of the house around $12,500.

Disaster struck. The results were an undesirable tenant and a clogged toilet. The first Roto-Rooter man who went down to clean it out informed me that the sewer tile was broken and would have to be replaced. The bid on that work was close to $1,000, and seemed like $10,000 to me. I began to wish I had never got involved in real estate investments!

Things got worse. The tenant got impatient, ran to the City Health Department, and I was summoned to come to the property. I did. I found three people from the tenants union with blood in their eyes, one representative from the City Health Department, and two from the City Building Department. They advised me that the house was unfit to live in and they would have to tack up their condemnation paper that very day.

To that point I had been arguing the merits of the building. At that point, I realized that was the wrong approach. I quickly reversed field. Rather than arguing, I asked them for time to make the needed corrections. Amazingly, their attitude changed as quickly as mine did. They softened and granted me the needed time. (As it turned out, the sewer line did not have to be replaced, a more experienced Roto-Rooter man was able to dislodge the blockage, and the City Health Department didn't press the other items.)

I had learned a lesson. I was shaken by the experience, and I was determined to sell the property as quickly as possible. One reason for my haste was that I was told if I sold to an owner-occupant, the city would not give them any trouble. I got rid of the problem property in about a week. It went fast because I sold it without any down payment. Remember that this was one of my poorer investments. But let's reconstruct what happened on the financial side of this investment.

First of all, the person who bought the home from me sold it within six months for a profit. A few months later, the second buyer decided to refinance it. When he obtained his loan, he cashed all the underlying contracts and mortgages out of the picture. When I figured up my return on the property, I was startled.

I had invested $700 on the down payment, plus $1,300 on improvements, for a total investment of $2,000. I had received $960 in rents after expenses and payment on the uniform real-estate contract.* I received an additional

*A uniform real-estate contract (called a land contract or just a contract in some states) is merely a contract between a buyer and a seller. These contracts can be ideal for both buyer and seller because of the flexibility both have in customizing terms.

$4,200 in capital gains, $350 of which was the amount the original seller agreed to knock off from what I owed him, in order to be cashed out from the second buyer's loan. The total income to me was $5,160 on a $2,000 investment in eighteen months! THAT IS A RETURN OF APPROX- IMATELY 172 percent. Keep in mind again that this was one of my poorer investments and one of the first when I really didn't know what I was doing. True, I had some beginner's luck, but the more deals you make and the more experience you gain, the luckier you become.

Two months earlier in that same year, by using the principles of leverage and forced inflation, I bought a small cottage on Sherman Avenue in Salt Lake City for $7,925. After spending $1,500 on improvements, bringing the total cost to $9,425, I secured a $12,000 first mortgage on the property, putting $2,575 in my pocket without any investment. The $1,500 improvements, changes anyone could make without specialized training, included basic- ally cleaning up and painting of the exterior, painting part of the interior, and adding a small amount of wallboard and some inexpensive nylon carpeting. My return on the investment? Well, it's not possible to figure as I didn't have any cash invested.

VERY LITTLE CREDIT REQUIRED

Many of the best buys with high leverage, epecially in small properties, can be made with uniform real-estate contracts. This usually gives the guy with fair to poor credit a break. With all the properties I have bought, only two sellers have checked my credit.

With these high leverage investments, one can see that it doesn't take much money to get started. Once you get started with several deals like this, you can have a fairly

good-sized capital base to move into the bigger properties
and into super leveraged situations, as outlined in Chapter
seven.

NOTES AND THOUGHTS

Notes And Thoughts

CHAPTER 7

SUPER LEVERAGE — SPRINGBOARD TO MILLION DOLLAR PROPERTIES

Conrad Hilton's mother gave her son this advice, "If you want to launch big ships, you have to go where the water is deep." (*Be My Guest,* p. 120.) Deil O. Gustafson, a man who is still virtually unknown and yet whose net worth is between $20 and $30 million dollars, knew that he also had to go into deep water in order to launch big ships. He also realized that if you don't have any money and still want to launch big ships, you must figure a way to do it. Like many others, he learned that big projects can be launched through the use of leverage. Quoting Mr. Gustafson, "Anyone who says you have to have it to make it doesn't know what he's talking about." He says, "If that [you have to have money to make money] were true, I'd still be back teaching school."

SUPER LEVERAGE WILL PUT CASH IN YOUR POCKET

When Deil Gustafson first waded into the water, he did it in a big way, using leverage as only the professionals and the most experienced real-estate operators would dare to use it. Quoting from the 3 January 1974, *Wall Street Journal,* front page, Gustafson's "first venture into real estate also was accomplished without the benefit of cash. In 1963, he and a partner, whom he has since bought out, learned that Nicolette Village, a development of 160 townhouse-type apartments in the Minneapolis suburb of Richfield, was available at a bargain price. He went to a bank in search of the financing.

" 'They asked me what I was paying for the property. I told them to go out and appraise it and tell me how much they'd put up,' he says. 'They did and said they'd give me $1.3 million which I guessed was 80 percent of what they thought it was worth. I said fine. The actual purchase price was $1.1 million. I used the $200,000 that was left to start some other things. It wasn't income, so I didn't have to pay taxes on it. When you're young and need funds, that's a great way to get it.' He says that the development has been profitable almost from the outset and that it's currently worth 'at least twice' his purchase price."

My definition of super leverage is when you buy a property and at the closing, or within a relatively short period after closing, you can take out all of your own equity money and have cash in what is sometimes called the "Hip National Bank," or your own wallet.

I have used the Deil Gustafson example many times in lectures and in consulting with people. Most are skeptical that such deals can be found today. I go on to explain the many deals that I've had with this so-called super leverage. Even after my explanation, most think I was as lucky as Gustafson in finding the deals. But I do not think it is possible for you or anyone else to go out and look at a hundred potential deals (possible purchases of income property) without finding at least three to five bargains. At least one and possibly two will be super leverage situations.

Now if you expect these super leverage investments to be labeled that, you are kidding yourself. If they were labeled "No-cash investment with a positive cash flow" or

"No-cash investment plus cash in your pocket of $100,000 or $200,000," they wouldn't last two minutes. No, they don't come labeled; it takes study, creativity, and some foresight. I said *some,* and I don't mean a lot. If you are a person of average or near-average intelligence, you will be able to make this kind of deal.

MY FIRST SUPER LEVERAGE DEAL NET $48,000

For example, in mid-1975 the Coventry Hearth, a twenty-two-unit apartment building, was brought to my attention by a real estate agent. This building had been for sale for some time. In fact, it had been listed in the real estate book that is published weekly. No offers had been made. Looking at the bottom line or net cash flow, it seemed like a poor deal, but the total price of $110,000 for twenty-two units was attractive. On closer inspection, it was quite apparent that expenses were extremely high and for the size of the apartments the rents were on the low side.

Realizing there was potential in the building, I restructured the income statement provided by the seller to see what the picture would be if certain changes were made. These were mostly cosmetic improvements in painting, carpeting, drapes, curtains, and a minor face lift. The result was that after improvements were made and expenses cut, the new cash flow would be extremely attractive. In fact, after those changes and all contingencies, the cash flow would be 27 percent cash return on my investment (down payment plus improvements). Of course, after I added equity buildup, put in an inflation factor, and added the tax advantage, the total return on my investment would be 47.8 percent (The inflation factor was only 2 percent.) Pull out your calculator and see what a beginning investment of $10,000 will do over eighteen years at a 47.8 percent compound rate. The results will surprise you.

As it turned out, this particular deal was even better than I had expected. To begin with, I bought the building for $102,000 with $10,000 cash, about what I projected, after three weeks of negotiation. Next, I found there were actually twenty-three units rather than twenty-two. The owner had been using one unit as a storage room. I spent an additional $25,000 (some from rents and some borrowed) in upgrading the building, everything from painting, carpeting, draping and face lifting, to landscaping.

At this point I had $35,000 cash invested in the property, not to mention many hours spent planning and arranging for the things to be done. With an overall return of almost 50 percent, should I be satisfied with my investment? Well, I was for a while. Then I looked at the situation again and saw a way to turn this attractive leverage situation into a super leverage deal. (Some brain compounding was taking place!) Let me back track and present all the facts in this, my first big super leveage deal.

Shortly after I purchased the Coventry Hearth and began renovation, including a change-over of 95 percent of the tenants, I found that the bad tenants were moving into the building next door, the Copper Crest. This didn't completely solve my problem because the undesirables were still in the neighborhood. As I moved new tenants in, the old tenants were harrassing my new tenants.

I approached the owner of the Copper Crest and explained the problem. He knew something was up because his problems had multiplied greatly in the weeks since I had bought my building. During this conversation, I found that he was in the insurance business and really didn't want to be a landlord. I asked him if he would consider selling his building. He said he wasn't interested in selling, and I let it go at that. He told me he would alert the manager to screen the renters more carefully.

A few weeks later when the problem had not abated, I approached him again with the same basic problem and the same quesiton: Would he sell his building to me? Finally on the fifth visit, he agreed to sell the building. I prepared an offer. Before delivering it, I called to tell him I had the offer ready. He had changed his mind and didn't want to sell. Since I had already prepared the offer, I told him I wanted to bring it to him anyway; and he agreed.

As I hung up the phone, I was in a dilemma. The offer I was about to present was a low offer because of the problems I would face in buying the building and unknowns that were ahead in the deal. However, I had expected him to counter with a higher offer that I probably would accept. Now that he had changed his mind and didn't want to sell, I didn't know how to alter the offering price for the building. I finally decided to keep the offer as it was and I delivered it to him, leaving before he had a chance to open it. (I wanted to give him time to think about it. Also, I didn't want him to read from me that I knew it was a low offer.)

Two days later he called me. I held my breath, wondering what his decision was. He stated flatly, "The offer looks fine except for a few minor points. Let's get together and discuss it." Needless to say, I was in shock, but delighted. I hustled down to his office and discussed what turned out to be very minor points. We both made some compromises, and he signed the offer.

The deal turned out this way: for the ten apartment units, most of which were one bedroom; a very nice office in the front of the building which he agreed to lease back from me at $500 a month on a five-year lease; and a small print shop in the basement, the total price was $90,000. Terms were $5,000 down and the balance on a twenty-year 8.5 contract.

So, from the purchase of the first building, I accidentally walked into a deal that did two things for me. First, the second building made it a super buy and gave me a fantastic return on my investment. Second, it solved the problem of the undesirable tenants being in the neighborhood.

As we closed the deal on the second building, a humorous situation developed. Upon finding that I was the purchaser of the building, the tenants who had just moved in from Coventary Hearth didn't wait to be asked to leave; they left, and in a hurry.

After the cleanup and repairs to the building, and change-over in tenants at an investment of more than $5,000, rents were increased enough to give me a 50 percent cash flow on my invested dollar and a whopping 88 percent total return on my investment!

For the seller, the deal was good also. The building had been a headache to him. It was a distraction from the insurance business he knew best and was obviously very successful in. A few weeks after the sale, he told me what a relief it was not to have the problems of the apartment building.

Now, with the two buildings sitting side by side and both giving excellent returns on the cash flow basis alone, I was receiving approximately $14,450 annually or an overall return of 32 percent on a cash investment of $45,000. Sounds like a deal that I would and should continue to hold just as it was. Of course, I could have done that. In fact, I could have held that property for the rest of my life and maintained the income by raising rents to keep up with inflation.

Depending on how high you want to rise and how aggressive you are, this is the kind of situation to try to turn from an extremely good deal into a super deal by using super leverage. That is what I am currently doing. This type of a deal can be found and consummated by following a few basic steps. (See Chapters 8 and 12.)

First, I approached the person who sold me the Coventry Hearth on a wrap-around uniform real-estate contract. The underlying or first mortgage loan was approximately $68,000 with me paying him on a $92,000 contract. In other words, his equity was $24,000. The terms of the sale were structured so that the interest on his $24,000 was accruing but would not be paid until the entire $24,000 plus interest became due and payable in five years.

My approach was to ask this man if he would discount what I owed him by $4,500 and take approximately $20,000 and subordinate his interest in the property in the form of a second mortgage, thus allowing me to put on a new first mortgage in the amount of approximately $120,000. He said he would not discount his interest by $4,500, but he would subordinate about $20,000 of what I owed him. The next step was for me to get the bank to make the first mortgage loan. OK, now what was my position when all this was accomplished? At the time that I received the $120,000 loan on the building, based on the new market price of $175,000, I paid the former owner $4,000 and executed a $20,000 second mortgage to him.

From the proceeds of the $120,000 new first mortgage loan, we deducted the $68,000 old first mortgage and the $4,000 prepayment to the former seller — the inducement to get him to subordinate his interest. (To subordinate means he would take a second mortgage position or a subordinate position to the first mortgage.) My position was that I had $140,000 in loans on the building and I had essentially a break-even cash flow basis, because the second mortgage loan was a short-term, five-year note. But the real bonus was that I had $48,000 in my pocket, $48,000 that I earmarked for an attractive investment in a $500,000 building.

Even without the benefit of forced inflation — increasing the value by improvements — this potential investment had a 20 percent cash flow, giving me almost $10,000 cash yearly on my $48,000 down, a $10,000 yearly inflation factor (or 2 percent on the total price), a big tax advantage, plus the equity buildup of approximately $5,000 annually, or an annual total return of about 50 percent on the $48,000, or $24,000. Remember that I still owned the Coventry Hearth, the first building. From it I received approximately $9,114 in benefits each year: $1,200 from equity buildup, $2,204 from inflation at 2 percent, and the balance from tax benefits.

Coventry Hearth Benefits

	Before Refinance	%	After Refinance
Cash Flow	$ 9,450	27.0	0
Equity Buildup	836	2.4	$1,200
Inflation (2%)	2,204	6.3	2,204
Tax Benefits	4,240	12.1	5,710
Total Return (on cash down payment plus improvements)	$16,730	47.8	$9,114

**Reinvestment
of $48,000 Cash
From Refinance**

$500,000 Building
$48,000 Down

	Dollars	%
Cash Flow	$10,000	20.0
Equity Buildup	3,000	6.2
Inflation (2%)	10,000	21.0
Tax Benefits	2,000	4.1
Total Return	$25,000	51.3

In summary, I gave up $16,730 in benefits from the Coventry Hearth (47.8 percent of my $35,000 cash equity) to receive approximately $34,114 in benefits ($25,000 from the new purchase without the benefit of forced inflation and $9,114 from Coventry Hearth). By implementing so-called forced inflation and increasing my equity at a faster rate, the benefits were much greater than the $34,114 I received without any improvements.

$60,000 NET FROM THE SECOND SUPER LEVERAGED DEAL

I approached the insurance man who sold me the Copper Crest with the same basic question I had asked the man who sold me the Coventry Hearth: Would he subordinate part of the interest he currently had in the building if I made certain concessions to him? The concessions I offered him were as follows: I would agree to pay him

$20,000 of the $85,000, reduce the pay off time from 20 years to 11 and increase the interest rate from 8.5 percent to 9.5 percent.

Additionally, I would make improvements and increase the value of the property, raise the rents and thus increase the value of the building even more. He agreed, and I proceeded with a first mortgage of $90,000 on the property. The cash from this mortgage was used as follows: $20,000 of the $90,000 went to the seller of the Copper Crest for the agreed prepayment. From the balance of $70,000, $10,000 was used to make the agreed improvements. This left $60,000 in my pocket to reinvest.

Bear in mind that the Coventry Hearth and Copper Crest were made into super leveraged deals at a time when bank refinancing enhanced their overall success. Interest rates have risen, mortgage terms have changed, and our whole economics environment is a new ball game. But basic success approaches such as super leverage remain the same. It is up to you, the sharp investor, to adapt your strategy to conditions as they are today. You can live with much higher bank rates but better terms must be negotiated with the seller—which of course can be done by finding a seller who is *very* motivated!

THE SKY IS THE LIMIT WITH THIS SPRINGBOARD

Do you begin to see how this so-called super leverage can be a springboard?

On the smaller properties, I get the contract or mortgage holder to subordinate his interest to allow me to put a first mortgage on the property. By using this method, you can get all or most of your equity out and still own the property. Besides putting extra cash in your pocket, this can give you some very distinct and large tax advantages. (See Chapter 13 on taxes.) Sometimes you can get more than your equity out and still own the property. These are cases where the person holding the mortgage or contract will subordinate his interest and his second mortgage, and the first mortgage you place on the property totals more than the value of the property. (See Chapter 11 on creative financing to show you how you can do this on your very first purchase.)

By using this type of creative financing and super leverage, you not only are able to generate cash for reinvestment, but you reduce your tax liability. You also do the impossible; you borrow second mortgage money at extremely low rates. As you probably know, second-mortgage money is expensive, 18 percent to 21 percent. By using this method of financing, you borrow second-mortgage money for as low as 8 percent or 9 percent. Of course, this depends on your original contract or mortgage arrangement with the seller and what you negotiate from that point. Using this method, I have had several situations where the second-mortgage loan was at lower rates than the first mortgage loan.

SWEAT EQUITY IS AS VALUABLE AS CASH

Arthur Cohen, mentioned in the last chapter, is a master of the art of creative financing. "Even when he cannot mortgage out [mortgaging out means completely financing out of a deal so you have no cash equity in the deal], his ideal is to minimize the amount of money he must put into a project. Cohen tries to limit his investment to his own efforts and creativity — 'sweat equity' as it is sometimes known in the trade.

"In Arthur Cohen's case, sweat plus leverage is the basis of his fortune. 'My greatest asset,' he says, 'was value and so generate all the capital I needed." (Laurence A. Armour, *The Young Millionaires* [Chicago: Playboy Press, 1973], p. 186.)

Quoting further, "The fundamental talent is the ability to select property that has a potential for an increase in value." (*Young Millionaires,* p. 186.) (In Chapter 8 you will see that the talent or ability to select properties with the potential to increase in value can be learned and duplicated. After you learn the basics and begin to apply them, you will be amazed at your success.) With creative financing (using super leverage and by the use of sweat equity being able to mortgage out of deals), you can continue to progress. When you get all your money out, you can go on to buy, and buy, and buy. The only factors that can slow you down would be your energy and your ability to find the deals.

You Can Follow Cohen If You Understand His Symbol

Cohen is mainly concerned with big deals now. However, he has held onto one small deal from his beginning years in the real estate business, because of its symbolism of what can be done, and what was done by Arthur Cohen.

"The love that Arthur Cohen bears for the Burroughs Building is something of a standing joke around the Manhatten headquarters of Arlen Realty and Development Corporation. It's a joke because the object of Cohen's affection is a one-story office building in the New York City suburb of Mamaroneck. The property earns only $1,500 annually — hardly worth, on the face of it, a passing glance from the chairman of a corporation that controls some $1.7 billion of U.S. real estate. In fact, the Burroughs Building isn't even owned by Arlen. It is one of

Cohen's private holdings, a leftover from his early real estate career, which he began with a $25,000 stake in 1954.

"But Burroughs is also a serious symbol of how he parlayed that stake into a personal fortune amounting to about $200 million. 'They laugh at me,' says Cohen, laughing himself, 'but I love that building.' He built the 2,300-square-foot property in 1957 without putting a penny of his own toward its $130,000 construction cost. For fifteen years he has received a steadily increasing income from the building, and to Cohen that kind of deal is what real estate is all about. Everyone at Arlen understands the symbolism. 'The quality on the return is there, and that is what I always look at,' Cohen explains. 'The little ones and the big ones are all judged on the same formula.' " (*Young Millionaires,* pp. 184-85.)

There are many, many super leveraged deals around both large and small in every city of the United States, regardless of size of the city. How to find these properties is the subject of the next chapter.

NOTES AND THOUGHTS

How To Master Your Financial Destiny

FINANCIAL FREEDOM REPORT

A monthly 64-80 page publication, by Mark O. Haroldsen

How to Turn $2,000 into $20,000 in Seven Months

Let me tell you about a young inexperienced man who dared to make a major money decision, even though he did not have all the facts to make that decision. (Rarely, if ever, do we have all the facts.) Joe Mirci, age 21, was a student and part-time janitor, working nights at Utah Power and Light Company.

Joe was a newlywed. He had recently returned from England where he had spent two years as a missionary for the Mormon Church. Joe had not had the advantages of a father since he was a teenager, so he had had to learn how to make at least some of his own decisions.

Started with Only a Dream

Joe had little more than a dream when he began — a dream and courage. Joe had the courage to make a hard decision. It was a big decision in his situation.

Problem: With a small income, should he buy an old, rickety building with the $2,000 he had saved working long hard hours, or should he "play it safe?" Joe could continue to struggle and hope to increase his income and savings as the years drifted by. (Joe had worked since he was a small boy, doing everything from pulling weeds to delivering newspapers.)

Decision: Joe made a tough decision. He made it quickly, after he had received some good advice and counsel.

Joe invested the $2,000 he had scrimped and saved to purchase that beat-up old building. Within seven months, Joe was in shock as he marched to the bank. He had sold that same property. His profit was an astounding $20,930 — all in cash and all his.

Prior to and during those seven months, Joe had come to me for my opinion on how to best manage and sell this building. In taking my counsel he was able to realize a tenfold return in a little more than half a year.

Schools Don't Teach Moneymaking

There are at least two lessons to be learned from this story: (1) You must make a decision; and in most cases, that decision must be made in a relatively short time. (2) To receive the best advice and counsel you can get, seek out and listen to those who are truly experts in the field you wish to pursue. (The cost of their advice will prove to be low compared to the rewards you will receive.)

Amazingly, throughout the whole world there is not one school, university, or college that teaches specifically how to make money, lots of it. There are business schools and colleges that teach the concepts and principles of business, but none (that I know of anyway) that gives a specific road map to follow. You can find several positive-thinking books that get you excited about arriving at your ultimate destination, but they also, fail to give a specific road map to guide you from where you are right now to your goal.

Judging from the hundreds of letters and phone calls I receive from people who have read my book, it appears that I have achieved, at least in part, my goal of generating both the excitement and the enthusiasm about the goal of financial freedom; and more importantly, the specific step-by-step procedure and road map to achieving that goal.

To Make Millions—Specific Directions Are Needed

Most of the phone calls and letters I receive ask for more directions. They inquire as to how certain parts of my formula could be applied to them—they ask for more specifics (some of the same questions Joe Mirci asked).

How to Master Your Financial Destiny
Financial Freedom Report

Since 1976, I have been constantly monitoring the needs of people like Joe Mirci. The answers to their questions that come up and the directions they need are contained in the 64-80 page monthly installments of the *Financial Freedom Report*.

The cost is $38.00 per year. Because of the thousands of subscribers to this report and the thousands that subscribe monthly, I am able to charge this small amount. And believe me, it is a small amount to pay for the vast amount of information that you will receive.

> I have been told by several clients that the *Financial Freedom Report* is worth far more than $38.00, because if the subscriber applies what is given him, the results of just one issue could pay for the whole year by one thousand times and more.

Salaries and Commissions Are Not the Answer

Take a few minutes right now and figure out how much money you will earn in your lifetime. You will find that it is really not very much. You certainly are not going to become a millionaire from your salary, wages, or even commission. By applying the principles and formulas in my book, combined with those in the *Financial Freedom Report* that, update and refine those formulas—plus answer those questions that always come up as you embark on your own program—you will be able to achieve financial independence.

Most People Will Not Buy This Report

I am sure the majority who receive this, even though they have bought my book, will not buy my *Financial Freedom Report* because of their lack of commitment. In fact, most people who read this announcement will put it down, thinking they will read and study it later. Why? Because they are not truly committed to their financial goals. Conse--quently,the average guy will not take advantage of this offer.

Wealthy People Are Decisive

I expect that. That is why the average person does not become financially independent. (One's IQ or education has little to do with it.) The individual who acts and dares to make a decision now—not tomorrow—is the one who ends up with the millions.

I am certainly grateful I had enough guts to make some of the $38 decisions when I started. (Believe me, some of them were tough to make.) They paid enormous dividends and have brought me much satisfaction, in addition to financial rewards. This has been so true that even now I wonder if it is really happening to me.

If You Have High Goals

You cannot afford NOT to invest in this report: That is, if you have set high goals—and I have to assume that you have or you would not have bought my book. Of course, some could probably achieve financial independence without my report. It would take much longer and you would no doubt make more mistakes.

You Bet I'm Trying to Motivate You

I have obviously been doing all I possibly can to motivate you to *action*. I have done the same thing for close friends and relatives. Why? Because I KNOW I can show you how to have absolute control over your financial destiny. I have done it myself and I know you can—if you will follow my formulas and instructions.

You and I Will Help Each Other

Sure, there is another reason I am trying to movitate you—to make money for myself. But this is good. That is what free enterprise is all about. Free enterprise is a system where I can benefit greatly—if you do. Believe me, both of us will benefit greatly.

What's in the *Financial Freedom Report*?

This is not an ordinary financial report. In fact, it should be called a complete course in achieving financial freedom. Each issue will vary from 64 to 80 pages in book-bound form. The report is designed to take you step-by-step to your financial goals.

In addition, here are some of the many other areas that will be covered in various future issues:

- Detailed Success Stories
- Latest Tax-Saving Ideas and Examples
- How to get money out of raw land and still retain ownership
- The Easy, Proven Way (with examples) to get started from scratch
- The Hows, Wheres, Whens, and Whys of Land Development
- More Workable Techniques for dealing with Banks and Other Institutions
- The pros and cons of Buying and Selling Land
- Areas of the country where bargains in income properties are plentiful
- Buying Bargains even when the market is tight (prices are high and much competition).

- New Twists in the use of High Leverage
- The Easy Way to Manage Property
- How to Persuade Sellers to Sell on Your Terms
- Locating and Motivating Buyers and Sellers
- Negotiating Better Bargains
- Buying in Small Towns versus Large Cities
- When Should One Move from Part Time to Full Time.

Dare to Make a Decision

I do not believe that a man or woman can made a $10,000, $100,000 or $1 million decision unless he or she has learned to make the $38 decisions. That is the decision you are faced with now. If you are going to make the decision, make it now. Act now. **Dare to make a decision.**

Two easy ways to order:

1. Fill in the coupon below and mail with check or money order payable to National Institute of Financial Planning, Inc., 1831 Fort Union Blvd., Salt Lake City, Utah 84121.
2. Fill in and mail coupon including credit card number, signature,and expiration date of your card.

Please put the date you purchased *"How to Wake Up the Financial Genius Inside You"* on the coupon below.

How to Master Your Financial Destiny
Financial Freedom Report

☐ One Year $38.00   ☐ Two Years $67.50   ☐ Three Years $91.00
    12 Issues   24 Issues   36 Issues

MAIL TO:
National Institute of Financial Planning Inc.,
Attention: Randy S.
1831 Fort Union Blvd., Salt Lake City, Utah
84121

☐ Check or money order enclosed
☐ VISA
☐ Master Charge

_____
(Name)   (Date Purchased Book)

_____
(Address)

_____
(City)   (State)   (Zip Code)

For credit cards, sign here: _____

Credit Card No.:_____

Expiration   Date:_____

Call for quick service 801-943-1280

NOTES AND THOUGHTS

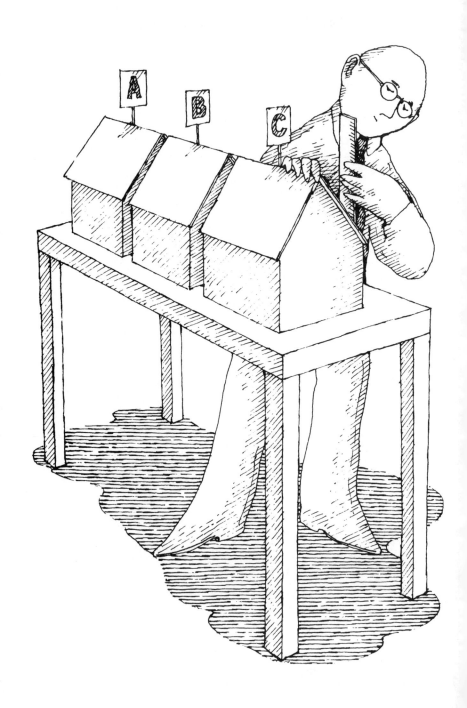

CHAPTER 8

TWO HUNDRED THOUSAND DOLLARS WORTH OF ADVICE

Remember Deil Gustafson (Chapter 7), how he found an apartment building, bought it entirely with borrowed funds, and put $200,000 in his pocket? Now the important question: Would Deil Gustafson have found the 160-unit townhouse development that he purchased for $1.1 million and taken out a loan for $1.3 million, if he had not been hunting? Of course not. Even if his luck had been phenomenal and he had come across that investment, if he had not been looking and hunting and comparing, he would not have *recognized* Nicollette Village as the remarkable bargain that it was. Opportunity would have knocked, but he would not have answered.

MAKE YOUR OWN LUCK

Countless times people have told me they wish they were as lucky as I was to find the super bargains I have found. Most of these people have not spent even one hour hunting for and comparing apartments, office buildings, stores, and other real estate investments. In fact, I can safely say that not one of these people, had they been offered any one of the super bargains I have bought, would have recognized it as being a bargain. The cause for this bargain blindness is that they have not spent the time shopping and comparing to have the knowledge it takes to recognize super deals. No, it doesn't take a lot of brains, but it does take experience and some knowledge. The knowledge can be acquired by any person with average intelligence. It doesn't have to come through formal education or even from books. (Books will save a lot of time, however.)

This knowledge can be acquired easily, but it will take time. You need to spend time shopping. You need to spend time comparing twelve-unit apartments with twenty-unit apartments, twenty-unit apartments with twenty-five-unit apartments, apartments on the east side with those on the west side, the north with the south, the good areas of town with the less desirable, and different apartments within each section of town. In other words, start acquiring and accumulating data and information about all sizes and types of apartments* throughout your city, and you will begin to understand what makes up value. If you compare at least one hundred different investments, you cannot help becoming an expert in determining value.

Then, when you come across an apartment complex like Mr. Gustafson did, you will quickly recognize it as a bargain. You will be so excited and anxious that you will not be able to sleep until you can present the offer. You will be eager to tell people about it, but you won't. You'll be afraid they will take advantage of the situation before you can. This would probably be a needless fear because most people would not have the knowledge or foresight to see it as a bargain. Still, to be on the safe side, don't tell anyone until the deal is sewn up.

---

*Note: There are many other types of income property, such as offices, stores, warehouses, shopping centers, and medical buildings, all of which can be excellent investments, but in the beginning steps of your program, it is highly advisable to stay with residential dwellings which can cover everything from single-family houses to a several-hundred-unit apartment complex. Also, tax advantages from the Tax Act of 1981 are weighted heavily in favor of residential income property, i.e., Recapture of Accelerated Depreciation.

Is all this work and effort really worth it? Let me ask it another way: Would you hunt, shop, and compare values in real estate investments if I paid you $100,000 for six months, or $200,000 for a year? Sure you would. And so would every other person in his or her right mind. But, you say, that's a sure thing. Well, that is exactly what you will be getting if you push yourself to do it on your own, if you work as hard as I would have you work for me in that six-month or twelve-month period.

GETTING STARTED

The biggest problem with most of us is how to get started. Vernon Howard tells about a man who is successful in many fields and who has the Midas touch that turns everything he touches to gold. Howard claims it's not the genius-like mind or the inside tips a person may receive or even a favorable nod from the goddess of fate. In an article entitled "$50,000 Worth of Advice," Vernon Howard says it is *making the decision*. Quoting from the article, Mr. Howard is telling how Arnold F. put it:

> Pardon me for saying so, but some of you have splitting headaches right now from trying to decide between Roquefort and French dressing on your dinner salad. Yet you call yourselves men of decision.
>
> Some of you are deciding yourself right out of everything you want. The plain fact is, you don't have the nerve to step right up and take what you want. You have the inner conviction that you maybe *could* achieve ten times as much. But you won't make up your mind to once-and-for-all go ahead.
>
> You rationalize by saying you'll wait until conditions are brighter.
>
> Or you thing you'd better think it over awhile longer.
>
> Or you don't think it's been done before.
>
> Or you say you'd better check with someone.
>
> Or you're not sure you can follow through.

Or you just don't know.

Some of you folks out there have more alibis than a kid caught in the cookie jar.

Maybe you are asking, "But isn't it intelligent to wait until I know exactly how things are going to turn out?"

The answer is, if you have to know exactly where you are going you will never go anywhere. That's the big problem. You want so desperately to be secure and to be protected that you're scared to step off into the adventure of the unknown. Go ahead if you want; be what you *call* secure. But don't ever expect to advance beyond the petty positions you now occupy. I'm not being insulting; you know I'm telling you the truth.

Personally, I rather enjoy the idea of not knowing exactly where I am going — that gives me the opportunity for investigation which can lead to improvement. Ladies and gentlemen, if you insist upon safety at every step you might as well close your doors and turn in your business licenses; you have no business owning one anyway.

Indecision is the mark of a fearful mine.

(Success Through the Magic of Personal Power, Vernon Howard [West Nyack, N.Y.: Parker Publishing Company, 1961].)

You must learn first of all that you must make a decision to get started. You must make a decision without all the facts, figures, and data to tell you exactly where you are going. Why? Because it would take more than a lifetime to gather all the data needed to weigh all the variables and possibilities that could happen along the way. There is no practical way to pinpoint accurately the final destination.

It seems to me that we have erred in our colleges and universities. We have placed so much stress on the importance of the technical aspects of business that somewhere, somehow, we have lost the total perspective. The emphasis is on how important it is to make finite forecasts, come up with sophisticated computer models, stress the need for complex calculations of risk versus reward, that we never get around to (or at best postpone ad infinitum) making definitive decisions, decisions we will stick by, decisions we will make work!

If you really want to make the $200,000 promised in the chapter heading, then take this advice: Make the decision to get started now. After the decision is made, the first step in earning that amount of money in a one-year period is one that is so simple that it sounds like a first grade reader. It is Hunt, Hunt, Hunt; Look, Look, Look; and Compare, Compare, Compare. There are no substitutes.

YOUR FORTUNE IS IN YOUR OWN BACKYARD

Now the logical questions: Where should you hunt? What should you look for? What should you compare?

The best answer to the first question is the oft told story of Ali Hafed who lived in ancient India. Ali Hafed was a wealthy man and very contented. He owned a large farm with orchards, green fields, and many gardens. One day a Buddhist priest visited Ali Hafed and told him an inspiring story about how the world was created. During that time, many precious metals and gems, including diamonds, were made.

The priest told Ali Hafed of the great worth of the diamond, even if the diamond was small in size. As he heard the story, Ali Hafed became discontented because although he possessed many riches and worldly possessions, he didn't have any diamonds. When he went to bed that night, he was a poor man because he was totally discontented.

The next morning he sought out the priest and asked where he could find these gems called diamonds. After receiving the directions, which were somewhat nebulous, Ali Hafed sold his farm, put his family in the charge of neighbors, and started his sarch for the diamonds with the money had had from the sale of his farm.

His search took him to Kenya, to Palestine, Europe, and Spain. In Spain, Ali Hafed, a poor, broken, disappointed, discontented man in rags, could bear the pain of his fuitless search no longer. He threw himself into the incoming tide and ended his life.

Back in India on the farm that Ali Hafed had sold, the new owner, while giving his camels a drink from the shallow stream, noticed a glitter in the bed of the stream. From the water he pulled a black stone that reflected the light with great intensity and displayed all of the colors of the rainbow. He took the stone to his home and placed it on the mantle.

Later, the same Buddhist priest came to visit this man in the former Ali Hafed home. He saw the stone and its bright glitter and asked if Ali Hafed had returned. He recognized the stone as a diamond. When he learned that the stone had been found in Ali Hafed's own back yard, he and the new owner rushed out and found literally handfuls of the beautiful stones. It is said that this was the discovery of the diamond mine of Golconda, supposedly the most magnificent and largest diamond mine ever discovered in the world.

The point is: begin your search in your own back yard. Start hunting for properties in the town or city in which you live. Whether it is 500 people, 500,000, or larger, you will find your acres of diamonds in your own back yard.

USE REALTORS FOR HELP

To enhance and aid in your hunt, you should enlist the help of Realtors in your city. Get to know the good ones. Ask friends for referrals of the brokers and agents of real estate who really know income properties. Don't stop with one or two; get to know dozens. Tell them the types of properties you are looking for. Let them know that you will look at properties at any time, that you are a serious buyer. When they call, be sure you go. Keep notes and glean all you can from the visit.

Use your local newspapers. Study the income property columns and the listings of single family units for sale. You will need to check dozens and dozens of properties before you will have the knowledge to recognize a true bargain. Before you have seen dozens and are in a position to judge for yourself, don't take the word of the agent or an owner as to whether a particular property is a bargain or not. Remember that his interest is different than yours, because he will benefit from the sale, whether he is the owner or the agent.

ADVERTISING PAYS BIG DIVIDENDS ($5 AD PRODUCES $45,000 PROFIT)

Second, use the newspaper to place your own advertisements. Start with simple advertisements, such as "Private party wants to buy older income property regardless of condition." Then just add your telephone number. At first, check out all leads you receive, even the obviously overpriced ones. As you do this, you will add to your warehouse of knowledge about properties. From such an advertisement as this, I purchased my first property, a twelve-unit, sixty-year-old building. I didn't have the courage to buy it on my own so I asked a friend to be a partner on that first deal. (He already owned about twenty units elsewhere in the city.) I made a shaky, low offer of $85,000 with only $4,600 down on a thirty-year, 6 percent contract. Much to our surprise, the owner accepted the offer without a single change. In fact, he accepted so readily and so willingly that we figured something must be wrong; we almost backed out of the deal. That would have been a big mistake. After some minor fix up and rent raises, the cash flow every year exceeded the original down payment. In fact, the cash flow was more than $5,000. (I bought out the partner a short time after the purchase.)

Three years later, with both forced inflation and natural inflation, the building was valued at more than $45,000 over the original purchase price. That little advertisement cost less than $5. Be sure to use this method in your hunt for real estate.

Tax Records: A Fast Easy Way

Another way to speed up the process and make your hunt more efficient is to use the city and county tax records to find out who owns what property. The people at your city or county building will show you the records with the names and addresses of property owners.

This source can be a most effective tool. Drive through the areas that have the size and type of buildings that would make the best investment for you. Say, for example, that you are looking for twenty units, about fifty years old. Drive around the area with those buildings in it. Write down the address of the building, plus a brief description of the property. When you have a list of fifteen to twenty, go to the records and get the names and addresses (some counties will give the information over the phone). From this point it is a matter of asking. Ask if they would like to sell. If the answer is yes, you begin to negotiate. (See Chapters 9 and 10.)

Ask And It Shall Be Given You

Lastly, the thing that will probably be of greatest assistance to you is your tongue. Ask people who owns a particular property. Ask people for referrals. Build a list of the names of those who own good income property. Talk to people who know people who own good income property. Most importantly, when you meet these people, *ask* if they would sell the property to you. The Bible states, "Ask, and it shall be given you." (Matthew 7:7.) Believe me, it works! Asking that simple question — would you consider selling your property? — has made hundreds of thousands of dollars for me. But you have to *ask*. Without asking, they will never answer, and you will never know if you passed up a bargain.

INGREDIENTS FOR A BARGAIN

The second question — what to look for — can be summarized in six short statements:*
1. Property that is undervalued.
2. Property that has potential for upgrading.
3. Property where rents are too low.
4. Property where expenses are too high.
5. Property where basic use can be changed (from apartments to offices, for instance).
6. Property that takes little cash to purchase.

*Since first writing this book I've learned through experience that probably the biggest factor to look for is a motivated seller. A person who wants to sell (for whatever reason) so bad they can taste it.

A combination of these six basics is desirable. The more of the six you have, the better off you are. Naturally. If you look hard, you can find deals with several of these ingredients. Remember, bargains are seldom advertised as bargains. You must learn to recognize them. I have found many bargains where the property needed upgrading, the rents were too low, expenses way too high, and little cash was needed. When you find bargains that are bargains from more than one of the basics, you have a good chance of upgrading them to a point where you can completely finance yourself out of the deal. This, of course, gives you all your money back, so you can do the same thing to another property. To do this, one must hunt. When you find such a property, you must recognize the potential it has and how to make the most out of that potential.

To the last question — what to compare — I would add, *why* compare. Here is a list of those things that you should compare.

1. Building cost per unit. Know and understand fully the building costs per square foot in your area so that when looking at a building, old or new, you have a point of reference to compare the building you are looking at with what it would cost today. Ask builders, appraisers, loan officers, and Realtors for the square foot cost. Get opinions from all so that you are sure that your figures are accurate.

2. Find out the value formulas used in your town. In addition to asking about building costs, take time to create your own value formula. I use rough rule-of-thumb figures for a quick appraisal to determine whether I want to pursue purchasing a particular building. Normally, I look at the gross income, net income, and rent for the size of unit compared with others in the neighborhood and the city. If rents are about market and the sales or asking price of the building is between six and six and-a-half times the gross annual income, it has my attention. If the asking price of the building is between eight and ten times the net operating income, this will also draw my attention. Remember that these are only general parameters and I would look further to determine if I wanted to pursue it to the point of making an offer.

3. Compare expenses. See what the rule of thumb in your city is and create your own formula for total expenses and the percentage of gross income. For example, I use a rough rule of thumb for expenses of around 30 percent of the gross annual income, assuming the tenants pay the utilities. (Of course, this will vary by area according to how expensive the utilities are.) If the utilities are paid by the owner, I use a 40 percent rule of thumb of the gross income for total expenses. Example: if I look at a building where my value formula of either gross or net compared favorably to other buildings in that neighborhood and where expenses were say $48,000 with a gross annual income of $80,000, it would immediately attract my attention. The reason, of course, is that it would be showing expenses of 60 percent of gross income. I would look closer to see why expenses are so high. If I found, for example, that the manager was being paid an exorbitant salary (I had one building where this was the situation), I would move quickly. Assuming that all other items were in line, I would make an offer, knowing that I could cut the expense figure from 60 percent to 30 percent or 40 percent ($24,000 to $32,000).

In today's financial market, the type and cost of financing are usually critical parts of the expenses and you will want to compare the figures of similar buildings. There are a lot of fancy formulas when it comes to financing a project, but I like to keep it simple. The one I use applies to the entire picture, not just to the financing part of the expenses. It is simply: What is the total yearly return percentage-wise of my cash down payment? As I compare all the aspects of a particular building with other buildings in the area, I place even more importance to my own requirements — to the total return I must receive from a building. The total return is cash flow plus equity buildup plus inflation plus tax advantages. This total must add up to a minimum of 30 percent per year; ideally, it will be a much higher percentage.

4. Compare price. Check what both the asking price

and the actual prices have been for apartments and other income property of comparable value. This information can be obtained usually from realtors. Most towns and cities have a multiple listing service that publishes both a record of properties for sale and those that have been sold and the actual selling price.

5. Compare the condition of different buildings. Look for and avoid buildings that have major problems (that would require high costs to correct), such as major structural damage, total rewiring, or a complete replacement of plumbing fixtures and drainage pipes.

Why compare? So you will learn to recognize a bargain when you come across it. Although it is good to know all the standards of comparison, the quick and almost foolproof method of analysis is to simply figure your anticipated overall return. Overall return can be defined as the total of cash flow, equity buildup, appreciation through inflation, and tax benefits expressed as the annual percent of your total cash down payment. As a rule of thumb, the absolute minimum you accept should be 30 percent. But don't hang everything on this one formula; be sure the quality of the investment is there. In other words, be reasonably certain that the return will be there for a number of years to come. If the building is in good condition, the basics are sound, and if your projections have been conservative for your city, rest assured that the quality of the return is there.

To make the advice worth $200,000, you must recognize that there are two types of bargains. First, there is the obvious type; the super low price versus current market prices. Amazing as it sounds, two identical buildings, side by side, often sell for drastically different prices, prices that vary 10 percent, 20 percent, or even 50 percent. So, for you to find a super deal, you must spend sufficient time hunting. You must look for those things mentioned above that make a bargain. Have a point of reference and compare values quickly. Then when you come across such a deal, you will recognize it and move quickly to make that deal yours.

The second type of bargain is the potential bargain or the sleeper. This type of investment has been around awhile, but no one has recognized the potential that you will be able to see in the building. The sleeper needs some new ingredient or a new combination of ingredients. The sleeper needs something creative to add value. Don't let the word *creative* scare you away, if you don't consider yourself creative. The type of creativity needed in real estate can be learned. Creative financing for example (discussed in Chapter 11) is easily learned and quickly imitated.

The types of creativity that make potential bargains into real bargains are simple remodeling, a cosmetic-type building face lift, cleaning, painting, fixing up, carpeting, and basically making the building a place in which people want to live; change of use to higher, better, and more productive use; and better management techniques that lower the costs of running the building and consequently increase the value.

Is it really worth it? Well, you answer it. Say you spent one or even two years doing nothing but hunting, looking and comparing. At the end of the second year, you came across that super bargain and bought it. Through your efforts and accumulated knowledge you were as fortunate as Deil Gustafson and you put $200,000 in your pocket. What would your answer to the question be?

Notes And Thoughts

NOTES AND THOUGHTS

Chapter 9

Set The Stage For More Than $100 An Hour

Your bargaining time, as you will learn in the next chapter, can be worth several hundred or more dollars an hour. Before your time can be worth that, before you can actually collect that much an hour, you must take the pains to set the stage to achieve those results.

The old times in real estate used to say there are three and only three rules for a successful real estate deal. They are (1) location, (2) location, and (3) location.

To this I say horsefeathers, horsefeathers, and horsefeathers. At one time this was possibly the law that led to success. But in today's market of high financing costs and mobile population, the rules have changed.

Key To Good Deals — Terms

Today's rules would be terms, terms, terms. In order to get those terms in the way you would like them, in the way that will benefit you most in the short run and the long run, you must take the time to preassess the situation. You will need to find out the seller's situation, so you will know how and where to bargain the hardest. Ask a lot of questions and listen carefully to the answers. If you are dealing directly with the seller, ask him the questions. If you are dealing through a broker or agent, ask the same questions and listen carefully to the answers you get through the broker. His answer will be what the seller is saying.

WHY IS THE OWNER SELLING?

What questions should you ask? Number one, find out exactly, and I mean *exactly,* why he is selling; be sure to listen carefully to his answer. He may say he is selling because he needs the cash. This indicates that on the surface at least he needs a lot of cash down or he might want to be completely cashed out. Don't be satisfied with that answer alone. Ask what he intends to do with the cash. In my experience, what the seller is really saying is that he wants to sell and take his gain because he knows he has one, possibly a big one. He is also concerned that the profit might not remain so he wants to cash in and be safe.

If you ask exactly what he is going to do with the cash, in most cases you will find that he intends to put it in an interest-bearing account, usually a savings and loan or a bank. At that point tell him that you understand his situation and that you think you can help. You can help by giving him a higher interest rate than he could earn from a bank or savings and loan. Next, ask specifically what rate he can achieve from a savings and loan or a bank. Point out that you can increase that by one or two percentage points. Then proceed to explain that by accepting a small down payment he can, by carrying the balance on a contract or a first mortgage basis, better his position by a substantial amount. Point out that his financial security is even better because he has a specific piece of collateral to guarantee that his position is safe. In most instances, this argument is convincing and everybody is better off.

BUY AT 20 PERCENT BELOW MARKET

By probing deeper, you will find out what the seller really wants. Then you are in an excellent position to do some hard-nose bargaining. When you finish bargaining and end up with a property at 20 percent less than its true value, with an interest rate 2 percent below market, you will agree that the terms are far more important than the location.

If, in asking why the owner is selling, you find that he needs the cash for a specific investment and that nothing but a large amount of cash will do, continue to pursue the questioning until you are satisfied that this is the real reason. If you find that, in fact, the seller does need all of his money in cash, this could be time-saving and beneficial information when you begin bargaining. (Chapter 11 on creative financing will show you how to structure an offer to meet the needs of this seller and give him the bulk of his cash on the deal.)

Bad Tenants Can Mean A Bargain For You

Think of questions that will give you an indication of how, from a management standpoint, the property is being handled. What you are trying to find out is whether the seller is fed up and wants to sell the property because of bad tenants and management problems. (This is the largest single reason for people leaving the most lucrative business in the world.) However, very rarely, when this is the reason, will the seller actually tell you his motivation for liquidating the property. If this is his reason for selling, there are several routes you may wish to take on proposing a deal. You must know with certainty his real motivations for wanting to sell.

In your questioning, find out what his tax situation is, not only on the property being sold, but his personal situation and the approximate tax bracket he is in. An offer to a seller who has a large profit and is in a high income-tax bracket would be much different than to someone in an average tax bracket, selling at a loss. Think through the tax problems of the seller, then make your offer so he will be in the best possible position. (In cases like this an installment sale is good for the seller; see Chapter 13.)

CAREFULLY PLAN YOUR QUESTIONS

Take time to figure out exactly how to ask these questions so that they are discreet, and so you will receive answers. Don't approach the questions with reluctance or from a negative standpoint; you probably won't get answers. Don't be like the securities salesman I knew in Denver, Colorado, who used to call people and say, "You wouldn't want to buy XYZ stock, would you?" After a short pause, he would almost always say, "Well, I really didn't think so, but I just thought I'd call and check. Nice talking to you. Goodbye." Plan your questions so they are positive and so you will receive answers to them.

If, for example, after probing, you found your stage was set as follows: The seller has large capital gains (long-term basis); has owned the property for six years (tax basis as far as sheltering other income has all been used); and is a person in the 50 percent tax bracket with little other shelter; then the bargaining point and the structure of an offer would be drastically different than to a seller who has small long-term capital gains; has only owned the property for 15 months so still has a lot of tax shelter left; and is in the 27 percent tax bracket. You must take the time to see the seller's position and what he really wants to accomplish. If you don't, you will be twisting the seller's arm as you bargain, and you may find out that you are twisting the wrong arm.

Take the time to check expenses, including taxes, and scheduled rent and rent rolls before you actually submit the offer. In some cases this is not necessary, as you should make your offer subject to the verification of expenses and gross receipts within a specified time (usually forty-eight hours) after acceptance of the offer by the seller. But by checking all expenses beforehand — especially where the expenses or gross rents seem out of line and are the basis of your interest in the property — you would be better able to negotiate and understand where to bargain hard. Taking time to do all this before the offer is presented will give you a great advantage over other competitive buyers. If you know rents are 30 percent to 40 percent low and costs can be cut by 10 percent or 20 percent, you may well jump at the seller's first price, recognizing it as a low price. I have been able to do this while my competition was trying to get an even lower price out of the seller. Knowledge of the seller's position usually makes the difference when it comes to the actual bargaining. And that difference can be worth thousands of dollars, so be sure you ask lots of questions.

NOTES AND THOUGHTS

NOTES AND THOUGHTS

Chapter 10

Be A Poker Player When You Bargain

A few years ago, a twelve-year-old, 100-unit apartment building was brought to my attention. After some checking, I found that the building had not been shopped — the real estate community did not know that it was for sale. I found out from the agent who brought it to my attention that I could only get more details on the building by making a special trip to the sellers in New Jersey.

Keep All Your Poker Cards Well Hidden

Having business in Washington, D.C., I decided to go on to New Jersey, especially since I had learned I would be the only one dealing on this property. After spending a morning in their office going over the books and records of the property, I sat down with the sellers to discuss price and terms. They were eager to have me make the first suggestion as to the price I would be willing to pay. They were, in effect, asking to see one of the cards in my hand. The poker game had started. I countered that since it was their building for sale, they needed to indicate a selling price before I ventured further. We played verbal poker for a few minutes longer before they mentioned the price of $1 million. I told them that sounded quite high, so I would have to study the figures carefully before I could talk price at all.

Four months later, after spending about 180 hours in

bargaining, we agreed on a deal at $850,000, $150,000 less than the seller's beginning price. A cursory calculation of the number of hours and the amount of money saved by bargaining, showed that the rewards for the time spent figured out to $833 an hour. Of course, this beginning price of $1 million and the ensuing drop to $850,000 would be meaningless if the price had been jacked up by $150,000 to begin with and the seller expected to drop by that amount. In this case, however, even the $1 million was a fairly good price.

By spending long hours bargaining and using logic and persuasive argument, the $150,000 saved turned an average deal into a super deal. Incidentally, the sellers in this case were certainly not dummies. They have thousands of properties throughout the United States. I did have the advantage of dealing in my own back yard and knowing the market I was dealing in. Also, I knew that I was the only potential buyer, so I didn't need to be concerned about someone moving in with a higher price. Even if you have competition on a deal, you want to bargain, but you won't always be in a position to hold out for the absolute bottom dollar. Many sellers try to use a potential buyer against another. Don't be bluffed.

Begin Playing With A Low Bid And Straight Face

When you start bargaining on a property, look at it as if you were playing poker. In other words, *don't* show your hand to anyone, especially the real estate broker or agent. If you do, your hand will be shown to the seller and the bargaining will be over. If you are trying to buy a property listed at $150,000 for $130,000, begin by bluffing. Begin with an initial offer of say $120,000 to $125,000, maybe even lower depending on the circumstances. (If the property is a bargain at the asking price, don't try to chisel.)

In several instances, I have made offers at a low price to bluff the seller and have had the offers accepted without a counter offer, much to my amazement and delight. When giving an offer to the sales agent or directly to the seller, don't ever show your cards by indicating that you know this is a low offer, that you expect a counter, or if the seller doesn't like the offer, maybe you can work something out. I heard one buyer say to the agent, "Gee, if I could get it at this low price, I would be tickled to death." That is tantamont to laying all your cards face up on the table as the betting begins, so everyone in the game can see exactly what your strengths and weaknesses are.

If you make statements like that to the agent, you can be sure they will be repeated to the seller, inducing him to make a counter offer at exactly what you planned on, or higher. However, if you make such an offer and send the agent along with the idea that that is your best shot, either it will be accepted (which, of course, is rare) or more likely (if your agent knows what he is doing), you will get a reasonable counter, probably very close to your targeted price of $130,000.

Since you will be speaking to the agent or seller when presenting the offer, take time to think through exactly what you are going to say and how you are going to say it. Otherwise, you may tip your hand and indicate what your feelings are. By the same token, listen carefully and ask probing questions to indicate the seller's feelings, attitude, and whether he will bend more. Entertain the idea of another counter to his counter.

Move Fast Only If You Have To

As in poker, don't get over-anxious, unless you know

that you are dealing on a super bargain and that there is another offer coming in. In cases like this, you may want to move ahead quickly, give up that bit of bargaining, and ensure that you have a deal. I had a case on a downtown Salt Lake property on which I was contemplating making an offer. I was waiting because it seemed to be the best thing to avoid letting the seller think I was too anxious.

The building was run down, had a lot of problems, and few people were interested in purchasing it. In fact, there had been absolutely no offers made on the building. (I found that out by asking.) While waiting for a respectable period of time to pass, I found that another offer was going to be presented. I quickly put my offer together and it was presented at the same time as the competing offer. The two offers were not even close. The other offer was trying to steal the building and was thousands of dollars away from my price which was also quite low. After the other offer was eliminated, the "poker game" the seller and I played for the next three weeks was indeed quite a game. He made a counter offer to my offer; I countered his counter; he countered my counter; then I countered his counter again; and on and on we went. In fact, this game went on all the way down to the day before closing. We were still debating, kicking back and forth who was going to pay the two-point loan fee for refinancing the property. (I finally won and he paid it.) What was all this poker playing worth?

Well, as it turned out, I saved 10 percent from starting at a low price. Not only that, but the terms of the deal were in my favor because of the long period of well-planned bargaining.

The only reason I could continue to bargain so hard and long on an already low-priced property was that the other offer had been completely eliminated. I knew that no other offers were being made on the property. In fact, I checked daily with the agent to make sure that he knew of no other offers coming on the property. Had I heard of any such offers, I probably would have curtailed my bargaining and quickly come to an agreement with the seller.

Whether a real estate agent is involved or not, your approach to bargaining should be essentially the same. The only difference when using an agent is that you are selling and working on him rather than on the seller himself. Remember, no matter how good a friend or close associate he is, don't show him all your cards.

The seller was obviously a so called "motivated seller" and that is the kind of sell you should always be looking for. The more motivated the better the deal you are going to come up with. You see motivated sellers will many times make "big concessions" that under "normal" circumstances they wouldn't dream of — so be sure to seek those kinds of sellers. Your check book will thank you.

Your First Deal Will Be The Toughest

Your first purchase, if you haven't already made it, is the toughest, mainly because, if you are at all like me, you will be extremely nervous and over-anxious to get on with your acquisitions so you can reach your goal. Remember, just like an over-anxious basketball player or other athlete, it is easier to make mistakes when you are in that frame of mind. Be cautious on the first deal. Look at it from all sides. Weigh it carefully. Don't move hastily, at least on the first one. If an agent is involved, he will, no doubt, bluff you into thinking that another offer is about to come in on the property. Think carefully of questions you can ask him to smoke out the truth regarding any other offers. In any case, don't let this rush you unduly to make too high an offer.

Unless you have made dozens of inquiries and inspections, as well as figuring many times the overall return on the investment, you may find yourself owning a property that was far from a bargain and that in no way fits into your investment program. This type of investment will not lead you to your goal. In fact, it will discourage you from continuing in your pursuit of a million dollars.

Although William Nickerson is talking about bargaining, purchasing of small properties (in this case, a single family home), his suggested method of bargaining is excellent. (These are market prices of many years ago, but his strategy is timeless.) He states:

How To Buy Property

Buyers and sellers who dislike bargaining may establish a firm figure and state, "That's my price. Take it or leave it."

When they do this in real-estate transactions they are usually left with no deal or a poorer deal than they could realice by tactful negotiation. After a certain amount of dickering the average seller, especially if his place has been on the market for several months, will accept an offer 25 percent under his original asking price, although he would refuse so low an initial offer. A competent realtor often convinces the seller to set a price near market value; so the broker's listing may already be considerably lower than the seller's initial asking price. Subtracting 25 percent from the asking price is of course no final gauge of value, since the knowing seller prices high to begin with. But we can use the resulting figure as a guide after checking other value factors. Discounting the listed price of $11,500 by 25 percent gives us $8,625 as an approximate target.

Before making an offer it is well to fix in mind the lowest price the seller might accept, then also set the top price you will pay, so that you are not apt to be swayed by subsequent sales pressure. In this case, discounting our target figure by about 5 percent to $8,200 would represent a bargain. Increasing the $8,625 about 5 percent to $9,000, the figure we arrived at when making our appraisal, would give us a good buy. To the target price about 10 percent might be added, making $9,500 our top price. If the offer is too low, the seller might shy off completely and refuse to negotiate without a higher starting offer. If the offer is too high, negotiations will be difficult to complete within the boundaries set. The first offer should probably be about 10 percent less than the $8,625 we aim for, rounded to $7,750.

How To Negotiate A Bargain

Make mental and written notes of defects, but don't point them all out to the Realtor as you go over a property. The agent can be better conditioned to negotiating a low price if the worst defects are enumerated as a prelude to giving an offer. You can be sure the salesman will repeat your knocks and add his own to pull the seller down. We tell Mr. Bokay the building is closer to forty years old than to the twenty he mentioned, since the inspection cards show it was built in 1926. We were looking for a place that needed fixing, but this is rougher than we had anticipated. The foundation looks bad, the way the porch is sagging. The place is badly in need of paint. To make it look decent some of the electrical and plumbing fixtures and all the furniture should be replaced. Instead of being worth the $10,000 the Realtor mentioned, the actual gross rents of $90 a month show that from an income standpoint, the place is worth only a base valuation of $9,000. And that figure should be discounted considerably to take care of the painting and other much needed expenditures.

Mr. Bokay expostulates, "Although I mentioned $10,000, that is pretty close to rock bottom. The owner is asking $11,500. The house is now renting for $90, it is true, but should rent for more even in its present condition. It might rent for as high as $200 if you fix it up. Besides, there is the full basement which could be converted into a new flat, and the two rentals could turn the building into a gold mine.''

We say that if we were selling we would expect to sell on the basis of the actual income, and that when we consider buying we apply the same yardstick. Any additional income that could be obtained would be eaten up by the cost of painting and remodeling, so all we can go on is what the building is actually taking in now. If the place can't be bought on that basis, we might as well forget it and look at something else.

Mr. Bokay tries to pin us down on how much we would pay. We say the place is probably worth a top price of $7,000, taking into account all the money that has to be spent on it. The agent repeats that he doesn't think he can get the owner below $10,000, but he finally agrees to write up our offer for $7,750. (*How I Turned $1,000 into Three Million,* pp. 74-76.)

DIFFERENT APPEALS FOR DIFFERENT DEALS

Variations should be used to this basic bargaining method. By knowing why the seller is selling and what he wants in addition to the position he is presently in, you may not want to bargain for a low price at all. For example, the situation of a person who is desperate for cash is drastically different than the seller who is in a high tax bracket and doesn't need cash. In the first case, a very low all cash offer using Nickerson's suggested method of bargaining would be the best route to go. In addition, where he is desperate, you would want to put a short-term fuse on it; that is, to close the deal as soon as possible.

In the second case, you may want to offer more than the property is actually worth to get attractive terms, and make a low down payment, possibly 5 percent or even lower. (You might need to show the seller you are a strong buyer so he will not risk getting the property back since he would be carrying the financing on the balance.) Or you may possibly be going for an extremely low interest rate of 8 percent to 9 percent. (Yes, I know the going rate is now much, much higher than this, but with enough negotiation and persuasion on your part, you can talk your way into rates as low as these.) (The seller would greatly benefit. See Chapter 11 on creative financing; also Chapter 13 on taxes.) By paying more than the property is worth, but getting it with a low down and low interest, your cash flow could be very high. Consider this type of offer if the seller is only concerned with his price.

Remember to listen carefully to the seller. Discover his wants and needs first. Then frame your offer and plan your bargaining around the knowledge you have acquired. By doing this, a high percentage of your offers will be accepted and you will move more rapidly toward your million-dollar goal.

How To Write An Offer Without Risking A Cent

The purchase terms are not the only thing you should concern yourself with when negotiating for a favorable deal. There are technicalities you should become familiar with. First of all, become intimately acquainted with the earnest money offer or deposit receipt, as it is called in some states. Study and know all about it. Ask Realtors to explain the different sections in it. Seek help from a competent real estate attorney, if at all possible.

It is a good idea to use an attorney at closing time, if you have not been through this process many times before. This could save you a great deal of money. I always make it a practice to put in plenty of "subject to's." These little additions in the earnest money offer give me a great amount of flexibility and have saved me from losing my earnest money if I didn't go through with the deal. These clauses are for your protection so that if things are not as represented, you have an escape hatch. The ones I usually use are "This offer is subject to the buyer inspecting and accepting the financial records and data of the seller within forty-eight hours after acceptance of offer." "This offer is subject to a complete inspection and acceptance by the buyer of the property within forty-eight hours of seller's acceptance of offer." It is also a good idea to put in the clause, "The seller warrants that all appliances, lectrical fixtures, and plumbing, heating and air-conditioning devices to be operative at time of closing." If the property on inspection does not measure up to what you expected, you can easily back out of the deal without losing a cent.

A Little Trick That Will Cut Your Down Payment

One other technicality that can assist the buyer and make it easier from a cash standpoint to purchase any property is the date on which the sale is closed. If the rents are collected on the first of the month, always try to close as soon after the first as possible, say on the fifth or so. This will make it so you, as the buyer, will not have to put up near as much down payment as was stated in the offer. That is, all the rents will be prorated. Since they will have been collected (the seller does this, insuring you from problems in hard-to-collect rent), the propration works in your favor. If you close on the fifth, the seller's portion of those prorated rents would be five days. Your portion, as the buyer, would be twenty-five days.

For example, if the gross rents were $3,000, the proration would work out to $500 for the seller, $2,500 for the buyer. The $2,500 would be deducted from your cash down payment which would in effect reduce your total investment in that particular property. Of course, if you are selling a property, you want to do it the other way around; that is, close toward the end of the moth if the rents are collected on the first.

Bargaining, dickering, and fussing over seemingly small technicalities such as the closing date can often make you literally thousands of dollars. It can also be extremely challenging, entertaining, and a lot of fun. As Conrad Hilton said, "I have played variations on that scene [the scene was bargaining] throughout my whole life, often with bigger chips, often over longer periods of time. But the rules are always the same and I have never lost the thrill of the game." *(Be My Guest,* p. 56.)

NOTES AND THOUGHTS

NOTES AND THOUGHTS

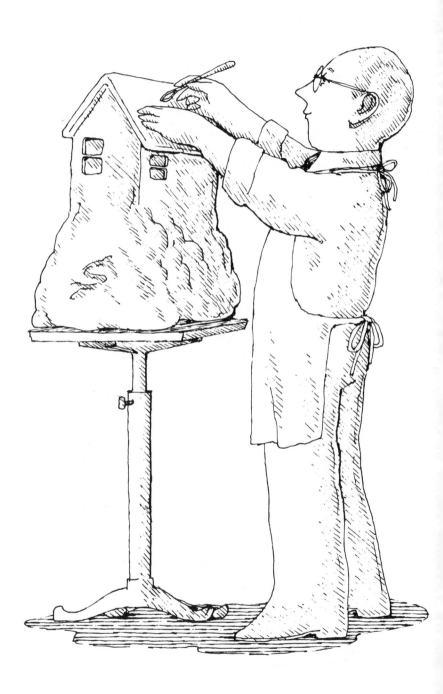

CHAPTER 11

CREATIVE FINANCING HELPS YOU BEGIN WITHOUT CASH

You can create miracles. It is amazing the miracles you can create in financing real estate, if you put your mind to it. This is where the brain compounding talked about in Chapter 1 really starts to pay big dividends.

While negotiating terms on a refinance package for the Coventry Hearth (the Coventry Hearth deal is described in Chapter 7), I began to see variations of my initial offer to the seller to refinance this building.

In my first letter to the former owner, I asked him to discount the $24,000 that I owed him by about $4,000. My concession was to pay off the discounted amount immediately instead of in four and a half years when it was actually due. He answered that he wouldn't do that, but with a large payment, he would carry back the balance on a second mortgage basis, allowing me to refinance with a larger first mortgage.

At that point the light bulb flashed on. There was the beautiful answer to my big problem (lack of excess cash to buy more properties) staring me in the face. It had been there all the time, but I hadn't seen it. His letter set off the series of events that would allow me to purchase in excess of $2 million in additional property.

After thinking through the idea to make sure there were no quirks, I wrote to all the people I had bought property from on uniform real-estate contracts or where the seller held the first mortgage himself. I made the same basic proposal to each one. I offered to pay part of the remaining balance owed them, increase the interest rate slightly, and shorten the payment period, thus giving them an incentive to accept the offer. Of course, my request was that they take a second mortgage position and allow me to place a new first mortgage.

The results were astounding. Letters and phone calls came back, agreeing to my terms. In fact, some of the responses were so enthusiastic that the amount of money I raised via this type of creative financing was around $200,000.

Using a couple of my examples, here are the details of how this was done. (Refer back to Chapter 7 for details on the Coventry Hearth package.) In a small outlying community in Salt Lake County, I had a modest income property (a single family unit). I had purchased it approximately fourteen months before. The price and terms were both attractive. I paid $1,000 down on the $8,500 purchase price with the balance of $7,500 on an 8.5 percent uniform real estate contract (land contract). The monthly payments were just under $90.

There was no question that this was an attractive price and a real bargain for me. (But, as you will see later, the method I am describing can be used even if you don't buy at a bargain price.) My letter to the former owner was somewhat as follows:

Salt Lake City, Utah
January 21, 1976

Mr. & Mrs. L. Somebody
Salt Lake City, Utah

Dear Mr. & Mrs. Somebody:

In reference to the property located at 2894 South 8900 West which you sold me in 1974, there is a possibility that, assuming you are interested, I could pay part of the amount owing to you and change the terms so you would be able to receive your money at a much faster rate.

Here is my proposal: I would pay you $1,000, which would leave a balance owing to you of approximately $5,326. That balance would be paid at $109.27 a month thereby cutting the term to five years, a reduction of almost four years and the rate would remain at 8.5 percent.

To make this change possible, you would need to subordinate your interest in the form of a second mortgage. Of course, if you still owe Mr. R.C., this would have to be paid at the same time or before we made our transaction.

If this would be advantageous and desirable to you, please let me know and I will take care of all the details to achieve this change.

Sincerely,
Mark O. Haroldsen

About a week later I received a phone call from the former owner. He was enthusiastic and said he would be glad to change his interest to a second position to receive the extra benefits offered him. I told him I would check on financing and get back to him within a couple of weeks. My next step was to go to a savings and loan association and secure a promise on a first mortgage refinancing.

I had to pay 11.5 percent, an extra high interest rate for that time (the house was in a less than desirable area and was an older house which most institutions do not like to finance). So after paying the $1,000 I had promised him, I put $7,400 in my pocket. (Of course, it went from my pocket into the bank to be used for acquisition of other properties.)

That capital *must* be reinvested or in no time at all you will find yourself swamped with debt and no assets or income from those assets to bail yourself out. Debt is a fantastic instrument if it is used carefully. If not, it is the most devastating of all the financial tools.

After the transaction was completed, my position was this: (1) I had $7,400 capital that I wouldn't have otherwise (it can work as leverage for me to buy a $75,000 property). (2) I had a property that was financed to the hilt and a little beyond. Cash flow wise, the property was slightly negative; that is, there was more cash being paid out each month than coming in. This is a bad situation in some cases, but not so in this particular case. Why? Because by using the $7,400 excess capital wisely, I increased the amount of cash flow over what I had with the former property. In essence, I ended up with a low-cost loan in terms of the cash I had to pull out of my pocket each month to pay for that loan. In addition, I continued to have the appreciation of the property through inflation, and of course, the tax advantage and an attractive equity buildup each year. Although the numbers are going to be different today because of interest rate, the concept is the same and is still working and will work for you.

A YOUNG MAN PUTS $5,000 IN HIS POCKET

Some years ago I was approached by a Realtor who had an opportunity similar to one you could easily find.

He had found a property that was a total disaster. Every window in the entire place was broken and the place was an absolute wreck. The price was ridiculously low, but the terms were wrong. The owner wanted a down payment, and the Realtor didn't have any cash. It seemed unworkable, but it wasn't.

My advise is so simple that it amazes me that more people do not use this easy method, especially in periods of high and tight financing.

Here is what I told him to do and this is exactly what he did. Make a full price offer to the seller with 25 percent cash down, the balance to be carried by the seller on a *second* mortgage, allowing the buyer to put a *first* mortgage on it at the time of closing. If the seller still insists on a larger down payment, you most likely can talk him out of it if you put a short enough term on the second mortgage.

In most cases, where the seller does not insist on all cash immediately, you can put this second mortgage for a longer period of time. The Realtor went out and secured a first mortgage to close at the same time he closed on the property.

The amount of the first mortgage was $10,000, $2,000 of which would be paid to the seller at the time of closing. (The total price was $8,000.) This left a balance of $6,000. But most important, this put $8,000 in the Realtor's pocket. He spent approximately $3,000 to fix up the property, but still had $5,000 to purchase other properties. It should be noted that after the house was completed, it sold for more than $20,000. It was this potential end result that convinced the lender to loan $10,000 on an $8,000 purchase. Even at first mortgage interest rates of 17 percent the debt service of approximately $150 monthly during fix up marketing and holding period makes sense.

BORROW $5,000 CASH AND OWN THE PROPERTY TO BOOT

But let's say you can't find a property that needs refurbishing and remodeling. How does this method of financing for raising cash work when nothing is done to improve the value of the property. You hunt for your miracle — a property that for one reason or another absolutely must be sold!

Perhaps there has been a transfer, a divorce, a death or an illness, or simply a landlord fed up with tenants. Now, in searching for the miracle property you must look for a property that is free and clear. Ideally, it should be the least expensive house in a good area (to bring up rental). Ideally it should need only cost-free upgrading, such as pruning, edging and yard clean up, window and wall or woodwork washing etc. Amazing what a few hours of carefully applied elbow grease can do to increase the rent structure of a neglected dwelling.

Let's assume you find such a property priced at $40,000 to $45,000. Because the seller is desperate, you agree to purchase the property for $30,000; $5,000 down, with the owner carrying a second mortgage for $25,000 amortized 30 years at 8.5 percent with a 10 year balloon. Most often the way to make this sort of purchase workable to both parties is to find a property that has been for sale a long time, is vacant and suffering vandalism, etc.

The owner must be desperate to sell. You will find many owners willing to subordinate their remaining interest, in this case $25,000, in the form of a second mortgage, just to be free of the worry. Since you don't have the $5,000 payment, you need to put on your offer that this offer is subject to your being able to find a suitable first mortgage loan at or before the closing.

Assuming with a good sprucing up you can rent this property for $400 a month and assuming that you had to pay a high price for first mortgage financing, that is, let's say 16 percent, here is the net result of the transaction you have just made.

Before the closing, you would have lined up a let's say, $10,000 first mortgage loan at 16 percent amortized 30 years (5 year refinance), or a monthly payment of $134, and a second mortgage of $25,000 amortized 30 years at 8.5 percent interest (see p. 133). Your monthly payment on the second mortgage would be $192. Assuming taxes and insurance of $30 a month, your total payment would be $356. And of course you have $5,000 in your pocket ($10,000 first mortgage less $5,000 down payment).

If you rented it for the $300, your cash out of pocket monthly would be $56. This is equivalent to borrowing $5,000 at 6 percent for ten years with a big bonus. That bonus is the ownership and control of the $45,000 piece of property which you bought for $30,000. Of course, this property would give you the additional benefits of tax shelter, equity buildup, and appreciation. In fact, with these three benefits, you end up in the position of having borrowed $5,000 at absolutely no cost to you.

The prime objective in this kind of creative financing — is to hunt for the desperate seller and then be bold about asking him to reduce his price and to subordinate his interest in the form of a second mortgage. If this all sounds mercenary consider the fact that you as buyer are presenting a desperate seller with the only plan that will work for you. You in turn have taken on a calculated risk in the 5 and 10 year balloons and in the higher rent projection. When he agrees, go to a financial institution, or to two or three of them, until you line up the first mortgage financing. This of course must be done before the closing. If you are paying over 10 percent for the first mortgage loan, in many states, the loaning institution cannot prevent the purchaser of a property from putting a second mortgage on.)

After you get the package financed, there are other things that you can do to make it attractive to you. For example, find a young couple who want to buy their own home. Sell the home to them without any down payment. Be sure you find a dependable couple who will stick with it, even though the monthly payments are higher than market. It will be easy to find such a couple, because it is simple to sell a property without any down payment.

Another alternative is, after you have finished financing the deal, to find a person in an extremely high tax bracket who needs tax shelter. Sell him a half interest in the property or all of it if you so desire. Of course, you would need to disclose all the facts.

There would be a negative cash flow but the benefits to him will be threefold. (1) A large tax shelter, which should be extremely attractive to him; (2) the equity buildup he would be achieving; and (3) increased value of the property through appreciation (due to inflation). If you sold all or part interest to an investor, you would do this for a nominal amount since he would be paying a high price for it. You would probably want to agree to manage the property so it would not be a problem to him.

What he would want from it would be mainly the tax shelter. The other factors — appreciation and equity buildup — would take time before the total value of the actual property would equal the amount of the loans against it. To get around this, you could agree to buy it back at a later date for the same or approximately the same price.

Whatever you decide to do after you have accomplished this creative financing, you will have $5,000 in your pocket ready for the beginning steps of reinvestment. You could do this several times, so your beginning base would be much larger.

A word of caution: since each such deal creates a negative cash flow, be careful not to overburden your financial position to the point that you drown. This type of leverage can be a tremendous boon to you and get you on your way in a hurry, but it also can be a millstone around your neck if not used wisely and cautiously.

You Can Still Get 8 Percent Mortgage Money

Get your nest egg started, whether through savings or through the method just described. Then, another method of creative financing, which can catapult you to even greater levels, is the use of 8 percent mortgage money which you can create.

If you buy a property and pay only 8 percent instead of 12 percent on a large mortgage or contract, your cash flow will obviously be much larger. This is because your total payment will be much smaller.

One hundred thousand dollars ($100,000) borrowed for twenty years at 12 percent would make your monthly payment $1100; whereas at 8 percent your payment would only be $836, almost $264 a month difference.

This $264 a month could allow you to buy the property for a price much higher than the asking price. (Many sellers will jump at a higher price with a lower interest rate.)

In fact, you could easily offer up to $30,000 more for the property and still be ahead. A mortgage for $130,000 at 8 percent for twenty years would make the monthly payments $1087, still $13 a month less than the payment for the 12 percent rate.

In addition, in Chapter 12 you will see how even $13 a month savings would add $1,300 value to the building. (If 8 percent seems ridiculously low to the seller, bump it up to 9 or 9.5 percent, whichever is acceptable to him and which makes a good deal for you based on the increased price. In 1979, I made an offer to a super-motivated seller of 3 percent interest on a $2 million property. He finally accepted a 7 percent compromise — originally he had asked for 10 percent.)

To take advantage of the 8 percent formula, here is what you do. Look for large income properties that are owned by older people. Usually this type of property is older. You will be looking for one that is free and clear. The ideal situation is one owned by a person in a high tax bracket, one he has probably owned for a long time, and if he were to sell it outright, the tax consequences would be devastating to him.

When you find the property, here is what you would propose. Offer to buy the building with a low down payment. This would be to the seller's advantage since the tax consequences to him would be minimal. (By selling it with a low down and on a long-term contract or mortgage, he will qualify for an installment sale. Installment sales spread the gain over a number of years and can reduce the total taxes drastically.) Consequently, he only has to show a small portion of his gain each year. (The 30 percent rule was done away with by the Installment Sales Revision Act of 1980.)

To make the offer even more attractive, offer a price somewhat above his asking price, but rather than pay him the 12 percent to 13 percent interest, offer him a 8 percent rate. Be sure to explain the benefits to him. Basically, the benefits are from a tax point of view. First, he is selling under an installment sale which gives him a big advantage. Second, by selling at a higher price and a lower interest rate, a larger part of the monthly payment will be going to principal than would have been with a market interest rate. So he saves money by paying capital gains tax (usually a lower rate than ordinary income tax) on a larger principal payment.

This method of creative financing can be used in more situations than the one described above; the seller doesn't have to be an older person with a free and clear property. Sometimes the seller would rather have a higher price with a lower interest rate for tax reasons, even though the underlying mortgage (when he sells on a wraparound mortgage or contract)* is at a much higher rate. Others will accept this type of offer just because they put a premium on selling price only and not on the terms of the deal. So give them their high price with low rate and you can have a much larger cash flow.

A 100 Percent Financing Idea That's Worth A Million

In his excellent book, *How Real Estate Fortunes Are Made,* George Bockl explains another creative method of financing.

> Here's a little known idea where you can get 100 percent financing when you show the lender how he can earn 17 percent interest while you're paying only 8 percent. Sounds improbable, doesn't it? Well, it isn't when you can find this set of circumstances, and it's not difficult to find, because it's fairly prevalent.
>
> Let's assume you're a competent young man with a good record in property management. You have found an owner of a sixteen-family apartment building who wants to

---

*A wraparound contract or mortgage is where a property is sold and the original mortgage or contract is kept intact. Payments are then made to the seller. The seller continues to make payments on the original mortgage or contract.

sell it to you for $200,000, subject to a $150,000 mortgage balance at 5 percent. But there is that clause that the lender can terminate the loan upon transfer of title, legal or equitable. It's a deal stopper.

Of course, you can't blame the lender for not being happy with the 5 percent interest, but there is nothing he can do about it as long as the original borrower owns the property. But here's where you can put an innovative leverage idea to work that is favorable to you and the lender.

Find the mortgagee who has the authority to make decisions, show him your managerial credentials, and tell him you are willing to sign a new $200,000 mortgage at 8 percent, the going rate, and cancel the $150,000 mortgage at 5 percent. What that means, you tell him, is that the effective rate of interest for the $50,000 he'll be advancing will be worth 17 percent. You don't need to explain too carefully that getting 8 percent on the $150,000 instead of 5 percent means 3 percent more interest on three times $50,000 plus 8 percent on the additional $50,000 adds up to 17 percent on the new $50,000 advance. The chances are he'll have it computed before you get through explaining it to him.

The only problem you may encounter is that he may not want to stretch his loan $10,000 or $15,000 to reach the $200,000 you request. But if you can convince him of your reliability and of your willingness to ride the loan without cash flow because of your prime goal to have a free and clear property by age sixty, then he would indeed be shortsighted if he turned you down. The chances are that raising the interest and the amount of loan will dry up all of the cash flow.

Your only risk is that you will have given the mortgagee a new idea and he may steer the deal to a friend of his who he may think is a more reliable vehicle for your idea. It's a risk you have to take, but it's not a great one, because most lenders are honorable men. If you convey a sense of integrity, he'll hold on to you because he'll respect you for your innovative idea, and because when he sees 17 percent, he'll act quickly.

Search for these situations. Every city must have hundreds of them. When you find a 2 percent or 3 percent interest spread which will give you an opportunity to leverage innovatively in a tight, high interest money market, move in on it. It's one of those remarkable ideas which enables the seller to sell his property, the lender to increase his interest yield, and you to ride in on a 100 percent financing plan.

Even if you consider yourself an ordinary salesman, if you can pull it off, it will turn you into an extraordinary one. ([Englewood Cliffs, N.J.: Prentice-Hall, Inc., 1972], pp. 202-203.)

As a variation to George Bockl's idea, try adding some second mortgage money. That is, ask the owner to carry some secondary financing. This will put cash in your pocket and make it 100 percent-plus financing. Of course, if you can't find one big deal, you can find two or three smaller ones and continue to find them until you have mortgages in excess of a million dollars.

Then all you need to do is sit back, manage the properties carefully and wait until the mortgages are paid off. If you are thirty years old or thereabouts and are able to sign your name on mortgages of a million dollars or more, and if these are twenty-five-year mortgages, you will retire at the age of fifty-five with over a million dollars worth of property. (This of course is assuming that properties do not depreciate any faster than the rate of inflation during that period of time, which is a very safe bet indeed.)

That is how simple it is for a thirty-year-old to become a millionaire by borrowing a million dollars.

Through the use of this type of creative financing, you can make seemingly unworkable deals into workable deals. You can turn small money-makers into large money-makers. You can put large amounts of cash in your pocket for reinvestment in bigger and even better deals.

The few methods described in this chapter are by no

means the limit to creative financing ideas. As you begin to finance your own deals, you will see new and better ways to fit your needs and the particular financial market at the time you buy and sell your properties. But like anything else, to make it work you must begin.

If you are cautious and have had no experience whatever in real estate, start with a small property. If you are not aggressive, would rather not use secondary financing, and you have saved a nest egg, then begin by finding properties you can buy with a low down payment. This makes your capital go further, and in each case you attempt to get the highest possible return on the cash you invest.

Later when you get more confidence, you can always go back to the people you purchased the property from (assuming the owner is carrying the financing) and suggest that they change their first position to a second position, thus allowing you to place a first mortgage on the property.

If you are aggressive, particularly if you have a little experience in real estate, the only things stopping you from making a million dollars are lack of ambition, drive, and the energy to apply the techniques outlined in this and other chapters. Remember what Conrad Hilton's mother told him when he was having a hard time getting started and taking big, aggressive steps, "If you want to launch big ships, you have to go where the water is deep." You can start in either shallow water or deep water, depending on the size of ships you are desirous of launching.

NOTES AND THOUGHTS

Chapter 12

Forced (Planned) Inflation Can Double Your Money Every Year

When I use the example of one penny doubled every year (see Chapter 1) or compounding at the rate of 100 percent annually, the majority of people do not think it is feasible or practical. I must admit I didn't believe it was possible for the average person when I started acquiring and improving real estate.

The key to achieving the goal of 100 percent compounded annually lies in improving the real estate. Had I not achieved the 100 percent goal so consistently, I would, even now, find it difficult to believe that it was an achievable goal.

The only reason I say this is because there are so many people who own income properties, apartments, offices, and rental houses, who have been in the business much longer than I have and still do not believe it is achievable because *they* haven't achieved it. These people are not using their heads to figure out how higher rates can be achieved.

Apply 100 Times Formula To Double Your Net Worth

If you understand and use the 100-times formula, you can easily double your net worth annually for many years.

100 Times Formula

$$1 \times 12 \text{ months } =$$
$$12 \times 8.34 \text{ gross rent multiplier } =$$
$$100 \text{ added value}$$

or

One dollar increase in rents or one dollar decrease in expenses per month is worth an average $100 added value to property. (That is on the average. In my experience the range is from $60 to $140 added value.)

By using this formula it is possible to spend only $10 per apartment and improve the apartment enough to justify a $1 monthly rent increase. By so doing, you will add $100 to the value of your investment. If you spend $100 per apartment and raise the rent $10 per month, you have added $1,000 value to the building.

Now it should be obvious how by the improvements you make to these buildings and subsequent rental increases, you will compound your assets at 100 percent per year.

Remember that with a 10 percent down payment, a 10 percent increase in value of that property equals a 100 percent return on your investment.

This theory is quite simple and the application is not much more difficult. Let's again use the simple example of buying a $100,000 property with 10 percent down, or $10,000. The balance of $90,000 is owed to either the seller or a financial institution or both. Through the use of forced or planned inflation, you increase the value of the property by 10 percent. The building is now worth $110,000 and the balance owing is $90,000, less principal payments you have made during the year. Your principal payments would approximate $600. (This would vary according to the length and interest on the loan.) The balance owing at the end of one year would be $89,500. Assuming there are ten units in the building, each rented for $225 a month, how can we actually make the building worth 10 percent more?

First, in order for a building to be more valuable, it must have higher revenues. In the case of an apartment building, it would be in the form of rental income. There are many ways to improve the value of a building and the individual apartment units to allow an increase in rents and keep the tenants happy.

The following list is only some of the ways. Any one or a combination of these improvements can be used. In each instance, we will not average more than $500 per apartment and will in effect have doubled our net equity within one year.

1. New carpeting. Assuming these apartments are approximately 550 square feet, we can add brand new high quality nylon carpeting at a total cost of $495 per apartment or $4,950 for the entire building. In order to get a high quality carpet for an average of $7.50 a square yard (it would take sixty-six yards of carpet to do 550 square feet), you must do some shopping. Check all the large carpet outlets telling each your situation, that you have apartments and will need a fairly large amount of new carpeting. Ask them what kind of a deal you can get as far as price. I suggest that you buy nylon carpet with the pad attached — a foam backed carpet you can have laid inexpensively. In fact, an average room of 12 × 16 feet can be laid easily in an hour. All that is needed in addition to the carpet is a good sharp razor and a staple gun. Merely roll out the piece of carpet, cut it to size, and staple it in place using a minimum amount of staples, mainly around the edges, through doorways, and a few in the middle. I stay away from carpets that do not show the dirt. In other words, tenants can go for weeks and weeks, even months, without vacuuming a carpet that hides spills and spots. This makes the carpet wear out much more rapidly as it will have to be shampooed more frequently.

2. Painting Interior. In an apartment 550 square feet, five gallons of good quality paint is sufficient to completely paint the unit. Be sure to get a high quality paint for which you will have to pay, even with a discount, between $8 and $10 a gallon. If you use a low quality paint, you will find that you will spend more for labor because you will have to paint it with two coats, in addition to painting the apartment oftener. On a per-apartment basis, you will spend about $50 in material and you should be able to hire an unskilled painter whom you can train for between $5 and $8 an hour, depending on the part of the country in which you live. This cost will run you $80 to $128 in labor for a total of approximately sixteen hours of labor. The total painting bill per apartment will be between $120 and $178 a unit or $1,780 at the most for the entire building.

Add to that figure several hundred dollars, depending on the size of your building, for hallways and common areas.

A word of caution regarding color. Don't try to get too fancy and get into color coordinating the different apartments with the carpets, etc. I did this for a while and found the cost, time and money rising rapidly as we tried to match different colors in apartments we had previously painted. Many hours were spent trying to match wall painting with furniture, carpets, and appliances. Stick with the basic colors, preferably light colors, white, off-white, or beige. You will save a lot of time, money, and headaches.

3. Drapes and curtains. In a 550-square-foot apartment unit, $200 or thereabouts will go a long way to improving the value of the apartment and the building, especially if you shop for bargains. Some of the large, discount chain stores, from time to time, liquidate large quantities of drapes and curtains. When they have such closeout sales, I have bought drapes that were regularly priced at between $20 and $30 for as low as $5 and $10 each. I haven't always needed drapes at the time, but the price was so attractive that I bought a large inventory of them to use in existing buildings or in buildings I have yet to purchase. I have purchased curtains at this type of sale (nice curtains with valances) for kitchens and bathrooms for as low as a dollar for the curtains and fifty cents for the valance. When you see such bargains and you think there are any you can use in apartments, be sure to stock up.

4. Furnishing the Apartment. I won't debate the merits of furnished versus unfurnished apartments and the prices you can get from them. But if you do have or are going to buy unfurnished apartments and are looking for an easy way to increase rents by 10 percent don't overlook the possibility of buying a few pieces of furniture. You will be able to increase the rent and make the apartment both acceptable and desirable for the tenant. A good queen-size bed, small love seat, a chair, and two or three beautiful pictures can enhance the worth of an apartment dramatically.

5. Improving the exterior. If the exterior needs to be made more attractive, this is where you should actually start improving. If not, then make the improvements inside that will give you the best chance of increasing the rents with the least amount of difficulty. In most cases, $5,000 spent on the exterior of a ten-unit building will go a long way to improving the value. If it is more than one story high, have a professional bid it and do the job. (Get at least three bids so you know you are getting a good price.)

By using any of these five steps, if you bought the building right, you can probably increase your equity two-fold. Remember also that one dollar in rent increases or expense decreases per month is worth an average increase of $100 in the value of the building.

By using any one or two suggested steps of improving the building's worth, we have kept our cost to $5,000 for the whole building's interior. If we sell the building at the end of one year, the net result would compound our money by 100 percent. We paid $10,000 of our own money and we put in an extra $5,000 to increase the value of the building to $110,000. This is accomplished by estimating before we began that by spending $500 per apartment, we could raise the rent by approximately $10 a month or $100 a month for the entire building which would equal $1,200 increased revenue per year and consequently a 10 percent increase in the overall value of the building.

After selling the building for $110,000 and deducting the mortgage, we have $22,700 left over, $5,000 of which was spent on improvements. So we have compounded our money by 100 percent because we turned $10,000 into $20,000. In this case, we actually did better than 100 percent, because we have not taken into account the cash flow which would have been approximately $1,000 during the first year, nor have we considered the tax benefits that would accrue to you had you bought this particular income property.

Remember, it is not only the *increase in revenue* that makes a property more valuable, but also the *decrease in expense.*

Expenses can be cut in many ways. I have cut expenses by doing everything from adding insulation to cut the heating bill (with fuel costs bound to continue to rise, this will be a big factor in the future), to cutting the garbage bill by reducing the number of pickups. Look at every expense with the idea of reducing it. Maintenance can be cut by having the manager do more. Insurance expense can be decreased by shopping harder and asking for a better rate. Management costs can be reduced by finding the right manager for the particular property. The electric bill can be cut by using electric timing switchers to turn off common area lights when not in use. These are just a few areas where you can save a dollar to add a $100 in value. Do some thinking and come up with more cost-cutting methods.

By using this formula, your profits will run wild. You will make more money than you, no doubt, thought possible. If you have the wisdom and self-control to reinvest those profits, you will create assets that will be enjoyed for generations.

Unfortunately, to the uninformed, making a profit, especially a large one, seems to be a bad thing. Even some well-meaning congressmen and senators talk about such things as obscene profits. I say unfortunate because this reflects a misunderstanding of the capitalistic system and why it is, and always will be, the best system in the world.

In the capitalistic system people are rewarded for seeking their own self-interest, but they are only rewarded if, while seeking to do the best for themselves, they also reward others.

John Deere, the man who made America's first steel plow, wanted to benefit himself; he wanted to sell the plow for a profit. It was difficult, at that time, because the superstition was that if you used steel to turn the soil, it would poison the soil. Deere proved otherwise, and made a fortune for himself. But look what the benefits were to mankind.

In modern times, look what has happened to the price of the electronic calculator. In four or five short years, the price has dropped from over $400 for a calculator that did the four basic functions to less than $10. Why? Because people who wanted to make a dollar moved quickly into the market to provide a calculator at a lower price, so they could sell more units and make more money for themselves.

The capitalistic system parallels the basic nature of man. That is, we try to help ourselves first. If we are smart, we see that by helping others we help ourselves faster. With this sometimes thought-out and sometimes subconscious plan, we proceed to help others with the ultimate goal of helping ourselves. Is this selfish? Possibly so, but is this kind of selfishness bad?

I have purchased income property with the intent of making a big profit. I see that the only way I will be able to do this is by improving the property and consequently improving the living conditions of the residents. When I raise rents, I expect to have a lot of complaints; even though I have improved the property and it is a much nicer place to live. The amazing thing to me is that I expect people to complain, but, for the most part, they don't. In fact, the comments and sometimes even letters from tenants almost make the cash reward secondary. Here is one letter taken from the *Salt Lake News* in January 1976:

Dear Sirs:

I would like to recommend the Coventry Hearth Apts., 454 South 5th East, as the most improved housing accommodations in our area. I lived there almost four years and in all honesty it was the most cockroach and mice-infested place I have ever seen. Most of the tenants were either using drugs or were alcoholics, and prostitution was also quite prominent, as was young men and women just living together. There were quite often violent episodes to the point where firearms were used a few times. Also the sewer and drainage facilities were neglected to the point that the smell was quite foul. The police and paramedics were there so often that a person could not keep count.

Mr. Mark O. Haroldsen bought the building and

though it cost him a huge sum of money, the Coventry Hearth has new furniture and carpeting, the halls and apartments have been repainted, the sewage and the drains repaired by plumbers, the insects were 95 percent eliminated by exterminators, and the undesirables have moved. They were not evicted and Mr. Haroldsen is not one iota concerned about discrimination. He is a good and patient man who tries to help people.

The main reason the undesirable tenants moved was because there was a different environment for them. They found that Mr. Haroldsen was a man who could not and would not allow himself to be manipulated or used. He was also a good example for us all, in the terms of how responsible people should be and by his personal manners. I strongly think he should win your award because of his achievements.

He has Chicanos, Tonganese and black people who are tenants there, and so far as I have seen no one has problems with their neighbors.

As an afterthought, we are also getting the green lawn into good shape for the simple reason that he makes sure it is watered and taken care of and sections of the lawn have been transplanted. As I mentioned, he has spent a great deal of money to accomplish this and it is not coming out of the taxpayers' pocket. It is coming out of his own.

Take it from one who has lived there for a long time and has seen the big change.

Sincerely,

Roy M. Gallegos

Editor's reply:

We took your advice, Mr. Gallegos, and gave the Coventry Hearth the award. And we are sure that Mr. Haroldsen agrees with us, that you must be a very special tenant to take the time and the energy to point out Mr. Haroldsen's accomplishments. We wish all of you real success in all endeavors.

People are motivated by a lot of different things. To me, there aren't many that are more stimulating than monetary rewards and sincerely expressed appreciation. I have found a great measure of both through my investments in real estate, and I know you can also.

NOTES AND THOUGHTS

CHAPTER 13

UNCLE SAM LOVES REAL ESTATE SO HE GAVE IT ALL THE TAX BREAKS

Remember Victor Posner, a man who is always working, who earns more than $170 an hour? At that wage, who wouldn't work all the time? Quoting from *Forbes Magazine,* 15 March, 1974, the article talks about Mr. Posner's collection of companies, D.W.G. Corp., Pennsylvania Engineering Corp., Universal Housing and Development, and NVF.

The article continues:

> The empire has one distinctive feature. It pays its emperor, Victor Posner, around $1,000,398 a year — which is $187,398 more than International Telephone and Telegraph paid Harold Geneen; $583,398 more than Ford paid Henry Ford; $595,398 more than General Motors pays Richard Gerstenberg; and $636,398 more than Exxon pays John K. Jamieson. In fact, Emperor Posner seems to be the highest paid executive in the land.

With such a tremendous yearly salary, you would certainly think that Mr. Posner would pay through the nose when it comes to tax time. But Uncle Sam loves Mr. Victor Posner because he loves real estate. Posner gets all the breaks that real estate affords. In fact, most of his income is sheltered. At least according to the same *Forbes Magazine* article which states:

> The real estate provided the initial financial base that permitted Posner to start acquiring public companies and

building up his annual income. Today the real estate may
shelter a substantial part of that $1,000,398 from income
taxes.

Sure, there are people who run around making a lot
of noise and complaining about rich people paying little or
no taxes. But it is the law and has been for a long time. It
was put there for a reason. The reason, of course, was to
stimulate investments in real estate and industry which
were and are in need of capital. We have heard a lot over
the years about tax reform and areas of tax shelter than
might be affected. But The Economic Recovery Tax Act
of 1981 resulted in the largest tax reduction package ever
enacted. Among the many benefits to the taxpayer, the
basic tax advantages of real estate have been greatly increased.

TAX LOOP-HOLES ARE FOR EVERYONE

The tax laws favoring real estate are for everyone, not
just for the rich. The Tax Act of 1981 had far-reaching effects that can benefit every investor. The basics of how to
take advantage of these new tax breaks are quite simple.
But you get more involved in real estate it will take more
expertise, and if you have not already, you will certainly
want to seek the help of a good tax accountant. There is a
lot of bad tax advice floating around, given by people who
are not informed. They often are trying to be helpful but
are doing more harm than good.

Be sure to seek out good, qualified, and experienced
professionals when it comes to taxes and tax laws.

In today's environment of extremely high taxes, the
tax consequence of any investment can be among the most
important considerations. Remember in Chapter 4 how
the wise use of tax laws decreased by *nineteen* years the
time it took to arrive at the magic million-dollar mark. It

is, therefore, obvious that you must look at and at least begin to understand the basic workings of why real estate is such a good investment from a tax standpoint, and how you can get the most mileage out of current tax laws.

When I bought my first income property, I had in mind making big capital gains. At the end of the first year, I was surprised and delighted in the large gain from several improvements I had made, if I had sold it then. But the real shocker was the added advantage the property gave me in the amount of taxes I would *not* have to pay, and the amount from other earnings that was sheltered.

TAX SAVINGS CAN BE MORE THAN YOUR DOWN PAYMENT

My down payment on that building was only $4,600. After improvements (paid out of cash flow) and after subtracting all other deductions from my income that year, Uncle Sam allowed me an additional $8,000 deduction because I owned this particular apartment building.

Believe me, at that point my opinion of the old Uncle, about whom in the past I had made disparaging remarks at tax time, changed drastically. It got even better when I found that I would have almost the same amount to deduct the following year, and a slightly lesser amount each year for the next five or six years. I began to dig deeper to understand all the ramifications of this kind of tax shelter.

TAX SHELTERS WORK QITE SIMPLY

The basics of what makes a good investment from a tax point of view are quite simple. Even though they are simple, many people do not understand, as was my case, just how tax shelters work. In fact, the president of a local bank, otherwise a very knowledgable man and a former bank examiner, asked one day, "Just how does this tax shelter thing work?" I took a few minutes to explain the basics, which he agreed were simple indeed. Here are some of the basics.

Any home owner knows that the interest he pays on a mortgage loan for his home is tax deductible for the year he pays such interest. With income property, not only is interest an expense that can be deducted (on income property, interest expense and the other allowable expenses are deducted from the income of the building), but there are many other expenses, including a big one that is really not an expense to you; at least, it is not an expense as far as cash out of your pocket. In our inflationary economy, it turns out that it is not an expense, but a blessing. That so-called expense is depreciation.

Everyone knows what the word *depreciation* means, at least, in the usual sense. It means reducing something in value. However, when you use the word *depreciation* related to real estate, it is more than likely true that it connotes an accounting expense only.

Depreciation is an expense that you are allowed to deduct from the income of the building after all other expenses have been deducted. Believe me, the depreciation expense can be a large one. Often after it is deducted, the property will no longer show (for tax purposes only, remember) a profit at all. In fact, it may show a good-sized loss. And that loss can be deducted from other income, including salary, wages, and return on other investments. In the following example* you can see that all operating expenses are deducted first, leaving a net operating income of $17,350.

*Note: The example uses the new 1981 Tax Act depreciation schedule. For properties purchased before 1981 the old formula will apply. See example at end of Chapter 13.

Apartment Building
Bought and Placed in Service after December 31, 1980
Income Statement*

Income (after vacancy)		$25,000
Operating expenses		
Taxes	1,500	
Insurance	300	
Utilities	3,000	
Management	1,800	
Garbage	250	
Advertising	300	
Supplies	200	
Other	300	7,650
Net operating income		17,350
Less annual interest payment (approx)		12,792
Gain before depreciation		4,558
First year depreciation		17,400
Total tax loss		– $12,842

*Note: This example is based on the following assumptions:

1. Purchase price $170,500
2. Down payment   20,000
3. Balance on mortgage or contract $150,500 at 8.5 percent for thirty years

From the $17,350, we deduct the interest paid on the mortgage for that particular year, which in this example is $12,792, leaving $4,558. Of course, if we want to figure the cash flow, we would deduct an additional $1,008, the approximate amount paid on the principal to reduce the amount of the loan. But let's forget that for a moment and deal with the $4,558 figure.

DEPRECIATION —
HOW IT PROVIDES TAX RELIEF

This next point is the entire crux of what makes a tax shelter. From the $4,558 figure we get to deduct, because of the new 1981 tax laws, the depreciation on the building for that year. Now remember, this depreciation figure is not a real expense in terms of cash, but only an accounting expense. In our example, the depreciation that we deduct is $17,400, giving us a total loss for taxes of $12,842. The $12,842 can now be deducted from other ordinary income from salary or wages, or it could be deducted from profits made elsewhere through investments or otherwise. That part, the $12,842, is what is known as the tax shelter. Now remember, in this example we will receive $3,550 in actual cash from the property and all of that will be tax sheltered also. ($4,558 less $1,008 paid on principal = $3,550.)

How exactly does one figure the amount of depreciation to be deducted? See chart on page 159. The typical income property is broken into four categories: land, building, equipment, and furnishings. First, you figure depreciation by determining the value on each of the four categories; the total must add to the price you paid for that particular property. Keep in mind that land cannot be depreciated, you will want to place the lowest true value on the land to get the best tax advantage. You must be realistic or IRS will challenge you, and you will probably lose. I suggest you consult your CPA or accountant as to what value to put on the land.

How to Figure Depreciation
According to the Tax Act 1981
Total Cost $170,500*

Percent of Total Price	Item	Value	Term (Years)	Amount of First-Year Depreciation
10	Land	17,500	—	—
71	Building	121,000	15	8,067
6	Equipment	10,000	5	2,000
13	Furnishings	22,000	3	7,333
Totals		$170,500		$17,400*

*Note: This example is based on the following assumption:
1. Purchase price $170,500
2. Down payment   20,000
3. Balance on mortgage or contract $150,500
   at 8.5 percent for thirty years.

How to Figure Depreciation
on Building in Service Prior to 1981
Total Cost $170,500*

Percent of Total Price	Item	Value	Term (Years)	Amount of First-Year Depreciation
10	Land	17,500	—	—
71	Building	121,000	20	6,050
6	Equipment	10,000	3	7,333
Totals		$170,500		$14,812

*Note: The $2,588 depreciation write off for a property that qualifies for the New Tax Act depreciation schedule.

There are several methods of land valuation. Probably the most widely used is derived from the tax assessment of the property. Another is the going market rate for land in the nearby vicinity. Choose the method most advantageous to you. Put as much value as possible on equipment and furnishings. They depreciate in a much shorter time which you can see by the chart is to your advantage.

As you can see, I put a 13 percent value or $22,000 in the furnishing category. (These furnishings would be mainly carpets and drapes.) According to the advice of my CPA, these items can be written off or depreciated in three years, which would give a deduction of $7,333 each year. The equipment and appliances normally could be depreciated on a five-year basis. The building itself, is written off in *fifteen* years. Thanks to the 1981 Tax Act, Accelerated Cost Recovery System, which shortened the "life" of real as well as personal property. Deprecable real property is now recovered in 15 years at 175 percent accelerated method unless the tax payer *elects* to use straight-line.

In the chart we used the straight line method. In straight-line, you take the value of the building, in this case $121,000, and divide it by the number of years of expected life, or fifteen. By doing the division, you get $8,067 yearly depreciation, with no "recapture"* consequence at sale or disposition.

The accelerated method of 175 percent would be easily calculated by multiplying 175 by $8,067 which is $14,117. But we will keep it simple and *elect* to the straight-line method. In this case, using the straight-line method, our total yearly depreciation adds up to $17,400. This is the amount that we deducted from the $4,558 figure to get our total tax loss of $12,842.

Let's carry the example further and see exactly what effect that would have on you and your tax position. We will assume that in 1982 you were married and had a net taxable income of $24,000. According to the New Tax Act Schedules you would pay in income taxes to Uncle Sam a total of $3,887. Now, in the example, if you had owned and placed the property in service after December 31, 1981, your tax would be as follows: $24,000 taxable income minus $12,842 from the tax write-off or accounting loss from your building which would leave you $11,158 as your new taxable income.

*"Recapture" is figured in when the property is disposed of. In residential income property the I.R.S. wants to get back everything taken in accelerated depreciation that is in excess of what straight-line would have been. In commercial property the I.R.S. recaptures *all* ac--celerated depreciation, ouch!

Simplified Tax Consequences
For a Married Man Earning $27,000 in 1982**

Before

Salary, wages and commissions	$27,000
Total personal deductions	3,000
Net taxable income	$24,000
Tax on $24,000 (if married)	$ 3,887

After

Salary, wages and commissions	$27,000
Total personal deductions	3,000
Net taxable income	$24,000
Less first year tax shelter from $170,500 building	-12,842
New net taxable income	$11,158
Tax on $13,746 (if married)	$ 898
Tax savings	$ 2,989

**The Tax Act of 1981 reduces the federal income tax rates for individuals, estates and trusts by approximately 25 percent over a 33-month period beginning October 1, 1981.

The tax on this smaller amount is only $898, or tax savings of $2,989. That tax savings is hard cold cash you would otherwise have had to pay in taxes. Remember, that is a low tax bracket. If your tax bracket is higher than that (and it wouldn't take much more income to be in a higher tax bracket), the effects of this investment become more dramatic.

Everyday thousands are reducing their tax considerably and thereby dramatically increasing their spendable income. His income was about $55,000 and, after deductions, his taxes were approximately $10,000, leaving $45,000 annual spendable income. He had other funds which he kept in a savings and loan drawing approximately 5½ percent interest. He took his money out of savings and bought a thirty-two-unit apartment building. By so doing, he reduced his taxes approximately $3,500 and received an additional $9,500 in tax-free income. In other words, his spendable income increased from $45,000 to $58,900 a year. As you might guess, he is becoming fonder of that East coast Uncle of ours.

If your sights are set high and you don't have a lifetime and a half to reach those goals, you must protect your investments from the ravishes of high taxes. New tax laws have increased that protection. But the shelter of cash flow from the investment and the protection it gives other income is not the only advantage Uncle Sam has given real estate.

HOW TO AVOID TAXES WHEN YOU SELL

He has given a big break when you go to sell your investment. If you have ever bought and sold a home that you lived in, you probably are aware of the tax law that allows you to sell a home at a big profit and buy another home without paying taxes on the profit from the first. There are a couple of conditions in the law, however. They are that (1) you buy a more expensive home that the one you just sold and (2) you buy the second home within two years after selling the first home.

With the sale of income-producing properties you cannot use the exact method, but there are laws that allow a similar action. That is, you can defer paying the taxes from your gain if you trade property rather than sell; and you must trade for a higher-priced property. Normally, it is difficult to find another property where the seller is looking for property exactly like yours. There is a way, however, to make a three-way trade, and you can buy the building you wish to buy and the seller of that building does not have to take your specific property as trade on his building. When you get to this stage of your investment program, get a competent and experienced Realtor to show you how this is done. Be careful to do it exactly as you are directed. One small mistake can kick it out as a tax-free exchange. Tax-free exchanges such as a three-way trade, are made daily in all parts of the country.

After you have acquired a lot of property and are ready to sell, your tax liability will be small if you use an installment sale. (When buying from a person with big tax problems, this can aid both of you.) An installment sale spreads the gain over a number of years. Prior to the Installment Sales Revision Act of 1980, you could not receive more than 30 percent of he total price in the first year in order to qualify. But the "30 percent rule" no longer applies and you may receive a large amount of the purchase price in the first year. Be sure to consult your tax accountant for the complete picture of your tax strategy.

I think you are beginning to see that Uncle Sam does love real estate and those who purchase it. But in spite of

this love, he has complicated the accounting expectecd on
each property. For this reason, I strongly advise that you
find a competent accountant or CPA. I prefer a CPA who
specializes in tax laws. By taking advantage of these laws, I
am advancing more rapidly toward my financial goals.

NOTES AND THOUGHTS

CHAPTER 14

MOTIVATION + FORMULA = SUCCESS

Belief, drive, desire, a positive mental attitude, determination, discipline, enthusiasm, excitement, and motivation are all vital ingredients of success. But each quality is only gas or fuel to power the vehicle.

Although a vital commodity, fuel is worthless without something to use it in. Belief, drive, desire, and the other ingredients of success must have the vehicle — a well thought-out plan — to lead one to his goal. After that, the proper methods must be used to execute the plan.

Motivation is the high-octane gas, and the plan or specific formula is the performance race car.

It is unfortunate that millions of those who want to enter the race of success in wealth have only one can of gas. To make things worse, many empty that can of gas into a dilapidated or unsafe vehicle.

YOUR FORMULA 4 CAR IS NOW READY

You, the reader, are standing there with a full or nearly full can of fuel. Do you realize that the vehicle I have shown you is capable of winning first place in the race? Only you have the power to dump the gas in, jump in and steer to the finish line.

Once you get going don't stop. It is your future and the outlook for real estate investment looks brighter than ever before.

U.S. News and World Report (October 12, 1981) headline an article with: "No Vacancy Signs Spread in rental housing." People who have given up on buying homes because of high mortgage costs are getting another shock: The tightest rental market since World War II. " . . . U.S. Vacancy rate is 5 percent—lowest rate on record."

Dow Jones and Co. financial weekly *Barron's* (September 28, 1981) quotes James P. Meagher of Balcor Co. (holders of 15,000 apartment units nationally) "apartment rents will double in five years."

In my opinion rental shortages will continue through the 80's.

THE FUTURE LOOKS BRIGHT — BUT YOU MUST MAKE A DECISION

In addition, many states and areas will benefit from increases in population, both from birth rate and the influx of people from other states. In Appendix C, you will find the U.S. Census Bureau projections of population for 1990. But even more important than these projections is your determination, your drive, and your desire to accomplish what you set out to do. With a strong personal determination, absolutely nothing can stop you. Without it, you will fail in the *best real-estate market* in the world. Regardless of how good your formula is, without the motivation and the determination to make it work, you have nothing.

Charles E. Jones has said many times that, "You must make a decision, make it *your* decision, and you must die by it." It is sad that few people can make decisions, and even fewer are willing to stick by their decisions, regardless of the consequences. Make your decision now, and make another decision to stick by that decision. When you apply the formula contained in this book, when you see that it works, don't stop there! Make it work again, again, and again.

Don't let your vehicle run out of fuel. Reinvest your profits so you can get the benefits of compounding. Later you will be able to spend huge sums without even denting your capital. But don't do that at first.

Even the Bible speaks of compounding and the good it can do. Read Matthew 25:14-30.

As you compound your money, don't forget to work on yourself. Increase your abilities through your own effort. Let your brain and soul compound at the same rate as your assets.

You Should Grow With Your Assets

On the wall in Lew Rosenberg's office in Denver, Colorado, hangs a plaque with this inscription:

> Why build these cities glorious,
> if man unbuilded goes?
> In vain we build the world,
> unless the builder also grows.
>
> — E. Markham

As you ascend the ladder of growth in both assets and personally, unless you also help build others, you really have not learned to live. You will no doubt end as the men in the story below.

In 1923, a group of the world's most successful financiers met at the Edgewater Beach Hotel in Chicago. Present were: the president of the largest independent steel company, the greatest wheat speculator, the president of the New York Stock Exchange, a member of the President's Cabinet, the greatest "bear" on Wall Street, the president of the Bank of International Settlement, and the head of the world's greatest monopoly. Collectively, these tycoons controlled more wealth than there was in the United States treasury, and for years newspapers and magazines had been printing their success stories and urging the youth of the nation to follow their examples.

Twenty-five years later, let's see what happened to these men. The president of the largest independent steel company, CHARLES SCHWAB, lived on borrowed money the last five years of his life and died broke. The greatest wheat speculator, ARTHUR CUTTEN, died abroad, insolvent. The president of the New York Stock Exchange, RICHARD WHITNEY, was recently released from Sing Sing. The member of the president's cabinet, ALBERT FALL, was pardoned from prison so he could die at home. The greatest "bear" on Wall Street, JESSE LIVERMORE, committed suicide. The head of the world's greatest monopoly, IVAN KREUGER, committed suicide. All of these men had learned how make money, but not one of them had learned how to live.

These men never learned to live. In fact, it is questionable whether they really learned how to make money, for they did not keep it. Don't forget the advice from *The Richest Man in Babylon*. These men obviously never learned the lesson from that story.

In learning to live as you go, you must realize that money is not the end product. It is only the tool that shapes, forms, and molds that product or goal. The goal is to build yourself and others as you travel along the path.

Never forget that those who are confused and think that money is the goal will end up like the men that met that day at the Edgewater Beach Hotel.

DON'T LOVE MONEY — LOVE THE GOOD IT CAN DO

Many people think wealth is bad. They quote the Bible that money is the root of all evil. But that is not what the Bible says; read it for yourself. "For the *love of money* is the root of all evil." (1 Timothy 6:10; [italics added].) That is the big difference. It is not the money that is evil; it is the love of money that ruins people. In fact, money is good, very good, if used for the right things.

Suppose for a moment that your child was blinded in an accident. You are told that his or her sight can only be restored by a very delicate and difficult operation. There is only one man in the world who can perform this intricate surgery. His services are expensive and it will cost $100,000 for the operation. Is money now good or evil?

What Is Money?

A great author and a great man, Sterling W. Sill, says this about money:

> Someone once said that money can't buy happiness, but his friend pointed out that it does enable one to pick out the particular kind of misery that he enjoys the most. Money may not buy happiness, but it's pretty difficult to be happy without it. It is hard to send children to school or to maintain a proper standard of living without something to use as a medium of exchange. Someone said, "Money ain't everything." His friend said to him, "Just name me three things that it ain't." Suppose that we name a few things that it *is:*
>
> 1. Money is the medium that we exchange for other things.
> 2. It is planning and industry made negotiable.
> 3. It is preserved labor.
> 4. It is stored-up accomplishment.
> 5. It is food, clothing, and education for children.
> 6. It is comfort and peace of mind for elderly people.
> 7. It may serve as the thermometer of our industry.
> 8. It may be used as the scorecard for at least one branch of our success.
> 9. It builds churches and fosters righteousness.
> 10. It has helped to win wars and preserve national security.
> 11. It has built comfortable homes and high educational standards.

12. It fosters research and helps to build up our national health.
13. Through money we may contribute to the welfare of other peoples.
14. By its proper use, we can multiply our own usefulness.

Through money one may store up the results of his own labor in such a way that it will go on working long after his own life has come to its end. With money we may send out missionaries, hold homes together, provide children with fulltime mothers, and do many kinds of helpful scientific research. (*The Miracle of Personality* [Salt Lake City: Bookcraft, Inc., 1966], pp. 165-66.)

Now implement the specific methods and formulas of financial success. Begin achieving your goals one by one, but also give plenty of hard thought and action to learning to live and enjoy life along the way.

YOUR GREAT OBLIGATION TO MANKIND

Build others with your wealth. Use your assets for good so your wealth will benefit the future generations. This is more than your task; it is your obligation. The eternal laws that govern the universe demand that you give more than you receive. You will receive in abundance, so prepare yourself to make even larger contributions to build yourself and mankind.

Notes And Thoughts

CHAPTER 15

FOCUS YOUR ENERGY
FOR STRENGTH AND PROFIT

The quickest route to any objective, be it monetary or otherwise, is to totally focus the attention on a minimum number of things. Thomas Edison was once asked how he was able to get so much done. He said, "It's very simple. You and I each have eighteen hours a day in which we may do something. You spend that eighteen hours doing a number of unrelated things. I spend it doing just one thing, and some of my work is bound to amount to something."

If Edison had taken the time to do a dozen unrelated things, the 1,093 inventions he patented would probably never have been invented.

AVOID SIDELINES

If you truly want to be outstanding in any field, there's one important rule you must observe: you must concentrate your energy and power. Get just one thing in your mind, your heart, and your bloodstream. Put side-blinders on your eyes, like they used to keep on horses to prevent them from being distracted.

With blinders on you'll be able to look straight toward your goal and forget what's happening on the sidelines. It's been said that sidelines are slidelines. You can't serve two masters effectively. Sidelines invariably take one away from his goal. Sidelines divert the attention.

They take away all your focus and instead of doing one thing well you do two things poorly.

That doesn't mean one can't have other interests. It means he can't have interests that divert him from his goals. The minute a second interest begins to compete with your goal is the minute you should drop that second interest.

Meshulam Riklis

Meshulam Riklis is a good example of how we can balance our interests. Riklis is a very successful man, having turned several small companies into the billion dollar Rapid America Corporation almost on his own. (The corporation is now worth over 2.3 billion.) Through a biographer, we get an understanding of a proper way in which we can share our business focus with other interests:

> "I have been accused of being like a racehorse with blinders," he once told me. "All I see or care about, they said, is the track ahead. Well, that might be a fine quality if I really had it. But the truth is I do get diverted."
>
> I see nothing to regret in being diverted from one's goal — that is, temporarily — if the diversion itself is worthwhile. I saw Rik "get diverted," if that is the proper phrase, during the Israel crisis in June of 1967.
>
> From the moment Nasser massed troops on Israel's borders and blockaded the Gulf of Aqaba, Rik plunged into the job of bringing assistance to the democracy that had for so long been his homeland. He headed a United Jewish Appeal Emergency Drive for funds among merchandisers. He poured his own money into the campaign and helped raise many millions more.
>
> And I saw Rik "get diverted" again when he helped organize a committee whose purpose was to rouse all Americans to strive for security and peace in the Near East. This was not a Jewish committee; its membership

was drawn from all faiths. Its aim was to protect *American* rights in the Near East — rights which might be completely lost if the Soviet Union's influence were permitted unchallenged sway among the Arab nations.

For it was not only disaster to Judaism that Rik foresaw if Israel were destroyed. Israel, an outpost of democracy, was a symbol of freedom. If it were annihilated (and some Arabs were still demanding this in the councils of the United Nations) freedom and democracy through the world would be dealt lethal blows. Rik flung himself into the struggle to avoid the holocaust. "Ask not for whom the bell tolls," he said to those he recruited for his committee. "It tolls for thee." And because he was right he was joined by scores of outstanding citizens representing industry, the professions, the arts.

These manifold activities, however, never interfered with the hours he devoted to business — which is why I say that in his case, as in the cases of many others, a primary requisite for financial success seems to be a dogged, single-minded dedication to one's job. Diversions come, yes; they are part of a man's social responsibility; but they cannot be allowed to interfere with corporate responsibilities. [From Oscar Schisgall, *The Magic of Mergers,* Boston: Little, Brown & Co., 1968, pp. 232-34.]

Passion And Objective

Even with his diversions, Riklis did not allow himself to become sidetracked from his ultimate objective. He was able to continue to focus his attention on his long-range goals.

Anyone will have a good chance of succeeding if he will concentrate his energies. But, on the other hand, if he divides his time and talents among more than one enterprise or goal, his chances of success diminish rapidly. The man cannot possibly succeed who allows chores, hobbies, politics, art, philanthropy, and other distractions or sidelines to steal attention and energy away from him.

A man's only passion should be his main objective. Once he lets the sidelines become his passion, he's lost, and that's the end of his dream.

THE LAW OF CONCENTRATION

Sterling W. Sill, in his book *How to Personally Profit from the Laws of Success,* explains how the law of concentration works:

"The doctor or lawyer or merchant or prizefighter who specializes is the one who invariably goes places. And yet every day we see persons who cannot resist the lures of the sideshow attractions. They still incline to the thought of cheating this powerful law by having sidelines and outside interests, and by that process they divide their power and subtract greatly from their effectiveness.

"Ralph Waldo Emerson wrote two essays on this subject. One is entitled 'Power' and the other 'Wealth.' The main theme in each is concentration. He said, in effect, 'Stop all miscellaneous activities. Do away with distractions, other duties, property cares, chores, errands, diverting talents, and flatteries — all are distractions which cause oscillations and make a good poise and a straight course impossible.' Distractions always untune us for the main purpose of our lives. Emerson said, 'The one prudence in life is concentration; the one evil is dissipation.'

"As a gardener gets good fruit by severe prunings, thereby forcing the sap into one or two vigorous limbs instead of allowing it to dwindle into a sheath of twigs, so anyone headed for some great accomplishment gets the best results by concentrating his effort in one place.

"A child may be perfectly content with his plaything

until he sees something that some other child has. The child usually wants everything he sees and drops one thing after another as new attractions are presented. We are very much like children. We want too many things and are not constant and faithful to any one thing. The Bible says, 'No man can serve two masters.' It doesn't just say that some can't; it says *no* man can. It just can't be done. You can't ride two horses in the same race. The Good Book says, 'Keep your eye single.' That means to keep just one thing in the focus of your vision. 'A double-minded man is unstable in all his ways.'

"The greatest Christian missionary said, 'This one thing I do.' That's why he became the greatest Christian missionary. A great Supreme Court Justice, in trying to indicate the value of concentration and how it had helped him achieve such a high place in the legal world, said, 'The law is a jealous mistress. It tolerates no competition. The law says to its devotees, "Thou shalt have no other gods before me." Success in any field says just about the same thing.'

"Singleness of purpose and an unwearied will give power greater than dynamite. It's a natural principle. We didn't invent the law and we can't do anything about it, but it is the law . . .

"We have only so many hours in a day. If we're trying to do four things instead of one, we can do two hours work on each instead of eight hours on one. But we always have to stop when we change directions. This means the loss of the great power of momentum. It also means we've lost the force and power and enthusiasm that comes from concentration.

" 'Jack of all trades and master of none' describes a human weakness of adults as well as children. We tend to want everything we see. If we take a fire hose and force the water out through the nozzle, we get great power. If we divide it into a spray, it falls softly with no force. The amount of sunlight that falls on the back of our hands is just pleasantly warm; but if we concentrate it through a convex lens and focus it into a pinpoint of light, we can develop enough heat to start a forest fire.

"It is really surprising how many capable men fail because they 'scatter their shot.' Some have sidelines. Others let numerous little cares destroy their success. I know of one potentially capable businessman who tends his own vegetable garden, milks a cow, takes care of his yard, does his own landscaping, paints the house when necessary, and does the plumbing. He runs the errands, does the shopping, carries his shirts to the laundry, and sometimes washes them himself. When his wife needs to go someplace, he does the baby-sitting. Each fall he puts on an apron and helps his wife bottle a winter's supply of fruit. He wipes the dishes and helps care for the children until he probably doesn't know whether he is male or female, businessman or handyman.

"This man thinks he is saving money, but actually he is wasting the most valuable thing in the world — the power of concentrated, one-directional, wholehearted effort. He also neutralizes his mind. He thinks like an errand boy and a baby sitter, not like a businessman. His mind is so occupied by this multiplication of little cares that it cannot cope with the important problem of becoming a success. He has even given up the peace and privacy and quiet of his own home by building an apartment in the basement. When the plumbing gets out of order, his renter just calls him; then he takes off his businessman's attitudes and enthusiasms while he becomes a toilet fixer. All of this brings the inevitable result: his wife teaches school to support him.

"This is an extreme case, but there are many people who are continually stumbling over a number of little diversions and spoiling their chances to succeed. They are always starting and stopping, always on the detours or sidelines, always trying to save a few dollars or earn a few in competition with the errand boy, the house painter, and the plumber. The bank president doesn't polish the brass or sweep the floor. If he did, he probably wouldn't be bank president very long. A businessman should learn to think like a businessman. His time is too important to compete with errand boys. He should not spoil a magnificent achievement by turning off the fire of his enthusiasm while he fixes the plumbing."

THE POWER OF CONCENTRATION

If you have an intense, unwavering determination to make your objectives and goals a reality, *nothing* can stop you if you can learn to concentrate your efforts. But that concentration is essential; you must learn to focus your attention on one thing, and keep it focused there, if you hope to succeed.

It's like the magnifying glass that Sterling Sill wrote of. With the glass you can take the gentle rays of the sun and bunch them together until the small shaft of light you've created burns a hole through steel.

When they're not focused, those rays of the sun are harmless. But focused through the glass they can exert tremendous power.

Many people have not set lofty personal goals, financial or otherwise. I have no quarrel with them; they can decide for themselves what they want out of life. Their reward will be in direct proportion to their goals.

But if a person decides to break out of this rut of *averageness,* he can't continue doing what the majority of the people are doing. For example, the average American family watches more than forty hours of television a week. The person who is trying to concentrate his efforts can't do that. He has to forego all that television in favor of his goal.

KARL ELLER

To be a great person — financially, artistically, socially, religiously, politically, or any other way — you must concentrate your efforts and attentions through that tiny magnifying glass. You must resolve not to be sidetracked by the hundreds of diversions that will tempt you — diversions that are sometimes interesting but are nevertheless usually meaningless.

Karl Eller is a good example of what we are talking about. He started out with a small mixed-media business in Arizona. Through a great concentration of power, Eller has built a company worth more than $367,000,000.

Eller's concentration has come much easier because he has believed in what he's doing. Years ago he was willing to bet everything that the billboard busines would grow like wildfire. He was somewhat of a pioneer in the field, but he had a vision of what it could become.

He stuck with his objective with the single-mindedness of a doctor performing surgery. Now his company, Combined Communications, has some 35,000 billboards in seventeen Western and Mid-western states. But he didn't stop there. His goal was to build Combined Communications into a billion dollar enterprise by the mid-1980's. He added five VHF and two UHF televisions to his company. Then he added the *Cincinnati Inquirer,* then the *Oakland Tribune.*

Eller increased his company's worth by $141 million in one year! Now he has merged Combined Communications with the Gannett newspaper chain, giving him almost $800 million a year in revenues, very near his billion dollar goal.

Eller was able to expand his company so quickly because he concentrated on a single objective. Most of his employees work long and hard hours, but few can keep up with their boss and his single-minded purpose. He works almost nonstop, and somehow manages to get by on only three hours of sleep a night.

Someone once said that John D. Rockefeller's genius was that he could concentrate all his energy, powers, and attention on one thing for five minutes. That may not sound like a great task, but just try it. In fact, try to concentrate your total mental powers on one thing for even sixty seconds, without allowing your mind to wander down any side tracks.

Not many of us can get by on only three hours of sleep a night. Not many of us have the concentrating power John D. Rockefeller is said to have had. But most of us *can* develop the power to concentrate on a general goal or direction — and by doing that we can become known for something great.

TRY IT FOR ONE YEAR

Give it a try. It's easily worth your time and effort. In fact, I would challenge you to concentrate all your efforts and energies on your goals for just one year. Mark on your calendar right now that for the next 365 days you're going to give single-minded attention to your objective. You'll resist distractions. You'll eliminate sidelines.

Oh, I know it won't be easy. Most of us find it difficult to say no when we're asked to help with some charitable drive — or when we're invited to visit our in-laws on a three-day weekend.

But go after your goal just the same. Try for the next

twelve months to eliminate all those things that divert your attention from your objective. Try to have a singleness of purpose.

Then, 365 days from now, look back and see what you've been able to accomplish. I'm convinced that you'll be able to do some great things just in that short period of time. In fact, one year of concentration on your goal will get you so deeply involved with it that nothing thereafter will be able to divert you from what you want to do.

Do you *really* want that goal? Then learn to focus your energy, learn to concentrate, and the goal will become yours.

Notes And Thoughts

NOTES AND THOUGHTS

CHAPTER 16

UNLOCKING THE SELLER

We all have a common concern: how to achieve the greatest financial return for the smallest financial outlay.

And in our attempts to find ever-more-profitable deals, we scurry here and there, running from one option to another, always looking for something better. Of course sometimes that's necessary. Sometimes we have to really hustle to get the kind of deal we want. (The willingness to go through the hassle involved in hustling sometimes makes the difference between the poor and the rich investor!)

But as we scurry about we too often miss the source of good deals that pays off more consistently than all the others. What is that source? The seller!

As I travel around making my own deals and hearing about others at seminars, this idea is supported time after time. Let me tell you of one experience I heard about.

A young man and his wife approached me and told me of their *first* investment purchase in real estate. It was a fantastic success — and the reason why was that they let the seller help them!

This couple bought an old hotel that was in pretty dilapidated condition, with the idea of converting it to an apartment building. With a lot of elbow grease and sweat, along with about $4,000 cash, they drastically changed the value of this property. Here are the numbers:

They purchased the building for $50,000 with $5,000 down, leaving a balance of $45,000. The balance was paid on an eight percent contract over twenty-five years, which made their monthly payment $347.32. By adding over 400 hours of long, hard work, they were able to convert this beat-up hotel into a respectable apartment building.

After completing their eighteen month project, they figured the building was now worth $170,000. How did they know that? Because that's exactly what they sold it for! In fact, they not only sold it for $170,000, but they were able to sell it with a $50,000 down payment.

So not only did they have all their cash back, plus a hefty cash profit in their pocket ($41,000 to be more precise) but they had a very nice income for the next twenty-five years, because the balance of $120,000 was drawing an interest of nine and-a-half percent. They were then receiving $1,048.44 a month for this piece of paper. So they were able to spend, save, or invest $702.12 ($1,048.44 minus $347.32) every month for twenty-five years ($701.12 × 25 years = total of $210,336.00). All they have to do is deposit the incoming check from the buyer and write a check to the person they bought the property from.

So you see, they were not only receiving nine and-a-half percent on their $75,000 equity ($120,000 less $45,000), but they were also making one and-a-half percentage points on the $45,000 since they were receiving nine and-a-half percent on the whole balance, and only had to pay eight percent on the $45,000 they owed to the person they bought the hotel from.

What does this story tell us about working with the seller?

First of all, more than anything else the key to buying bargains today is expressed in those two words: The Seller. The seller can be the key to bargain financing, bargain prices, and bargain terms. Always, always, always look to the seller first, for all of the above three. Later on, you can try for a superleverage deal by talking the seller into subor-

dinating his position behind another, larger first mortgage. Again, the seller is the key. If you have financed
with a bank, there's very little likelihood of superleverage.

Because of their initial approach with the seller, this
young couple was able to go from being in the property
business to being in the finance business. Because banks
have been so ridiculously tight with loaning money on old,
fix-up type properties, enterprising people like you and me
need to get into the financing business.

How can such financing work? If this couple had
done nothing more than turn around and sell the property
the very next day for the same price, they could have made
money by charging a higher interest rate. (They could have
made $16,875 in twenty-five years by selling the property
for the same price, but with a nine and-a-half percent interest rate.) But they were even wiser than that. They put
in "sweat equity" as well as some cash equity to improve
the property drastically.

Then when it was time to sell, they again acted wisely.
If they had insisted on someone refinancing it, they might
still be holding the property, looking for a bank to
refinance it. But by taking back the paper (selling the property on a contract and in essence lending the buyer some
of the financing) themselves, they not only have a sizable
and continuing income for the next twenty-five years, but
they were able to sell the property quickly.

So there is benefit in selling smartly, as well as in
working smartly with the seller when you buy. Take some
time to study the amortization book, which really should
be your financial bible, so you can structure deals both on
the "buy" side and the "sell" side. If you do, you'll move
yourself more quickly along the road to financial freedom.

Looking back at my best deals, I must admit that my
time was most profitably spent studying the amortization

book to see what my payment would be with various lengths of time and amounts of money. (If you don't have an amortization book by now, you should get one.) Your time both as buyer and seller, can well be spent studying its contents.

NOTES AND THOUGHTS

NOTES AND THOUGHTS

Notes And Thoughts

CHAPTER 17

HOW TO RAISE $200,000 IN TWENTY-FOUR HOURS

A few years ago when in the growing stages of my real estate acquisitions, I came across a super deal in a residential home. It was a magnificent four-story home built high in the mountains among the pines. It was built to look like a castle with an interior floor plan and design to fit a king. It had five fireplaces, several bathrooms, a fantastic den and library, and was designed with all the extras and luxuries one would want in a home. It was to be sold at a foreclosure auction at the county court house at noon. I found out about it three days before the auction was to take place.

I desperately tried to raise what cash I thought it would take to purchase the home. (At foreclosed property auctions, they generally require a cashier's check for most, if not the entire, price bid.) I was able to borrow $50,000. It was extremely difficult to do because I had not laid enough groundwork prior to this because I had no way of knowing that I would need that amount of cash so quickly.

I went to the auction and found to my surprise that there was only one other person bidding on the property. To make a long story short, the other person outbid me and picked up the property for $60,000 which was only a fraction of what the property was really worth. It is obvious from this story and many others I could tell, the value of putting your hands quickly on large amounts of cash.

In addition, you should take note of the fact that only

two people showed up for the auction. If I had been the
only person who showed up for the auction, I could have
bought the property for $1 over the mortgage.

Literally dozens, maybe hundreds of super bargains
are available every day in your town or city. Two ingredients are necessary to take advantage of them, and both can
easily be available to you. First, you obviously need to
know about such bargains and deals. This will come as
you make more contacts, and keep up contacts with people in the real estate business. You might think that
Realtors would scoop up these super bargains before they
show them to you; in most cases, that is a needless worry.
The second ingredient you must have in many cases to take
advantage of these bargains is fast and liquid cash.

Many people have had such opportunities presented
to them where quick cash was necessary. Most were unable
to take advantage of the opportunity because of a lack of
cash. A simple process is available where you will be able
to generate quick cash within twenty-four hours. It is a
many stepped procedure, it will take time to lay the
groundwork, but it is easily executed.

For lack of a better name, I call it the "banking round
robin." Go to several banks in your area, preferably in the
same day or within a two-day period. The number of banks
you contact is up to you and depends on the amount of
money you feel you might need. I keep accounts in a
minimum of ten banks, from each of which at this point in
time I am able to borrow $20,000 on my signature. Take
with you to each of these banks a statement of your net
worth.

Armed with the ammunition of your financial statement, approach the commercial loan department and tell
them that you need a $1,000 signature loan for thirty days.
Of course, depending on the amount of your statement, the

$1,000 request may be much higher on your initial visit to the bank. As a rough rule of thumb, many banks will lend up to ten percent of your total net worth on an unsecured signature loan.

Repeat this process at as many banks as necessary for your needs. Using a round figure of ten banks, at the end of this first step you will have borrowed a total of $10,000 — $1,000 from each bank.

It is usually suggested, if not required, that you set up a checking account at each bank from which you receive a loan. In most cases, I do this before I request the loan: I can then tell the bank that I am one of their customers. When setting up a checking account, request the unnumbered checks. This way the account will not cost you anything to set the account up other than a nominal monthly charge for carrying the checking account.

With the $10,000 you have generated from these loans, if you do not have immediate use for the cash, I would suggest that you deposit it in another bank in an interest-bearing account, if possible.

Thirty days later, when the notes become due, be sure they are paid on the thirtieth day not the thirty-first day. If you request and bargain for a good interest rate, you should not have to pay more than two or three percentage points above the prime lending rate. (To find the prime lending rate, call any stock brokerage firm, preferably a member of the New York Stock Exchange.)

Wait approximately sixty to ninety days. Go back to each of the banks from which you borrowed an initial $1,000. This time request a larger amount, depending on what you think the banks will loan, maybe $2,000 or $5,000 or they may only lend you another $1,000 at this time, depending on your financial statement. Request a longer pay-back period this time — a ninety-day note instead of thirty days. If each bank approves a $5,000 loan, you would be able to raise $50,000 in the second step.

The "banking round robin" concept is nothing more than continuing this step-by-step process. Each time you go to the bank, ask for a larger amount and a longer payback period. What you are doing, of course, is establishing good credit by repetition. That is, you always pay back the money when it is due, and by being prompt combined with the number of loans you've made and paid, you will have established a good credit rating and relationship with the institutions.

Of course, the amount that the bank will lend you will vary depending on the size of your assets, which are probably a lot more than you realize.

A variation to this method, and I should point out that there are many variations you could use, is to apply for credit at twice as many banks as you actually accept loans from. For example, if you applied for credit from ten banks for $1,000 each and then accepted loans from only five, after thirty days, assuming you needed that $5,000 on a particular investment, you could borrow $5,000 from the banks that you initially did not accept loans from.

By using this method, you could actually borrow money and never pay it back out of your own pocket. You could continually pay back loans with other loans; your only cost would be the interest incurred. Some might consider this a highly aggressive or unsound way to finance. You should be aware that this is precisely what our government has been doing for several decades. Our huge national debt will no doubt never be paid off.

When the money becomes due periodically, all that the government does is issue more bonds, notes, and other financial instruments to borrow money to pay off the old debt. Many corporations do the same thing; they borrow money to pay off old loans. Then at that future due date, they borrow again to pay off that loan.

As you continue to execute this program, you will find that your credit rating will become stronger and stronger (assuming that you always meet your obligations on time). The result will be that you are able to borrow more and more money.

Of course, you *must* use the borrowed funds carefully. *Repeat: only use such funds for investments and appreciating assets.* If you do this, you will be using leverage as it was meant to be used.

Remember that leverage can be the best tool in the financial world or the worst. It can eat you alive or it can make you a millionaire, depending on your ability to make sound and wise judgments.

NOTES AND THOUGHTS

Notes And Thoughts

CHAPTER 18

QUANTITY: THE SUCCESS QUALITY

"Lucky Ted Williams!"

That's a sentence that's been repeated thousands of times. After all, the guy grew to be 6'4", weighs 210 muscular pounds, and has great eye-hand coordination; in short, he's a born hitter, right?

Glenn Tuckett, athletic director at Brigham Young University, knows Williams personally.

"I've seen Ted Williams stand in front of a group and absolutely pound the podium, he was so mad," remembers Tuckett.

" 'Lucky Ted Williams!' he would explode. 'There's no such thing as lucky Ted Williams!' Then he'd go on to tell how he learned to play baseball."

When the custodian arrived each morning to unlock the school, the air was hushed and cool with that early morning feel. The sun was beginning to dry the dew; birds were chirping. Quiet and uninhabited? No, the boyish Ted Williams had arrived at the school playground, even before the janitor.

Ted was there swinging his baseball bat, hitting the ball — again and again. At recess he would rush to grab his bat, go out to the schoolyard, and hit some more. At noon he gulped down his lunch and was out in the hot sun for more practice.

Other kids went to the park after school to daydream or talk. The Williams kid went to the park after school to practice some more hitting. He practiced so much that his hands often blistered and bled. Glenn Tuckett remembers what Williams said, ''There's never been a guy who hit as much as I have.''

Sports authorities are fond of arguing the heredity-versus-environment theory. Is it background or training that makes a good athlete? When it comes down to it, most believe that great athletes, including homerun hitters, are born. Ted Williams is enraged by that, too. ''They're 'born' all right — after 2,000 hours in the batter's box!'' he fumes.

''You see,'' explains Tuckett, ''he was saying that 2,000 hours of hitting is the gestation period. Only then can a good hitter begin to grow to greatness.''

Of course there are many prerequisites for success in any field, but again and again in successful people, and Ted Williams is an example, we see one quality.

According to the law of probability, a man who buys a thousand lottery tickets has that much greater chance of winning than the man who only buys one. So Ted Williams, even though he had undeniable natural talent, was not content to buy just one ticket in the success lottery. Or ten. Or even a hundred. By his own estimate he paid as high a price as anyone ever has in order to *increase his odds* for winning.

''Ted Williams is as great a hitter as anyone who ever lived,'' says Glenn Tuckett. ''If his career hadn't been interrupted by four years in the military service, he would have set even more records than he did.''

Anyone who wants to be successful should absorb the *numbers game* into his life. If you want to be a success, you must be willing to make the necessary investment.

The numbers principle applies, of course in every aspect of life. Take book publishing, for instance. Erich

Segal taught at Harvard for years, and prepared some scholarly research articles.

In a sudden turnaround, he wrote a sentimental, romantic novel. He sent the book of to a publisher and awaited the reply. It must have been galling to receive a noncommital rejection notice from that first company.

There are undoubtedly thousands of authors, unacquainted with the *numbers game,* who pack their stories away forever after one rejection notice. Segal, however, sent his novel on the rounds of the publishing houses.

In all, that novel was turned down many times before Hollywood discovered it. The novel was made into a film entitled *Love Story* and was published in book form as well.

The film was a box office sensation and made its delighted author a regular fixture on television talk shows. Needless to say, *Love Story* made a lot of money for Erich Segal. He had been willing to make the numbers investment. He made not one try, but dozens, in order to *increase his chance* for success.

Even fishermen rely on the numbers game. On 4 March 1977, Bob Bringhurst of LaVerne, California, his brother, and their father got up before dawn and launched their fishing boat into the cold waters of the Flaming Gorge Reservoir in Wyoming. The three men were trolling an area of the water known as Sheep Creek Bay. Bob had just let his ten-pound test line, baited with a three-hooked gold rapalla lure and hand painted to look like a rainbow, into the water, when it was struck.

Bringhurst set the hook and began to work the fish, reeling in carefully. The minutes ticked away. In the boat, excitement was building. This was one big fish! Using all his skill, Bob played the fish for ten to twenty minutes, his heart pounding, before he finally landed.

Aboard the boat, the thrilled Bob Bringhurst surveyed his catch — a beautiful brown trout, fully forty inches long and twenty-five inches around! The men sped to the marina and then to the grocery store. It was only 6:40 a.m. and most of the world was still asleep.

They finally found signs of life at the Manilla post office, which in this fishermen's hamlet was equipped with an official scale. Thirty-three pounds and ten ounces! A world record lunker!

Many a fisherman dreams about that kind of a trophy mounted in his den. Bob Bringhurst had done more than dream. He had made the investment that *increased his odds* for success. He has made four or five extended fishing trips each year — a couple to Flaming Gorge Reservoir and the others to the High Sierras. He has not missed opening day in years. Any free time Bob Bringhurst has, he can usually be found fishing the lake near his home town of LaVerne. He is consummately interested in fishing.

Here are three entirely different examples: a professional sport, a bookish project, and an engrossing hobby. Each is different from the others, yet the same numbers principle contributed to the mastery of all three.

Before being named athletic director, Glenn Tuckett was head baseball coach at Brigham Young University. His experience with hundreds of athletes has led him to generalize that about ten percent of them are sparklers. Like Ted Williams, they have the character traits to make them stars.

Another ten percent he describes as those who "have memorized every excuse there is for losing." He believes the same percentages extend out of the sports arena into the rest of life. As evidence, he points to results of Korean brainwashing of American prisoners of war. Only about five percent of the men captured seemed to be independent minded. The rest were relatively easy to influence. He extends the Shelley quotation to say that athletics and any other endeavor of life are "through time and change unquenchably the same."

What then about this great majority who comprise the remaining eighty percent? Tuckett's prognosis for them is good. They may not have learned about the rules for success yet, but his experience tells him that this eighty percent can learn to be consistent winners.

Take the example of Johnny Huart, for instance. In his junior year at Notre Dame, he was a rather ordinary football player. He only made the traveling squad for one field trip, and played a very unspectacular seven minutes at quarterback during the entire season.

One of the eighty percent? Definitely. Yet Huart determined to make the numbers investment required of a standout player. Countless grueling practice hours, grinding hours of learning tactics, hours and more hours of building strength — all improved his chances for success.

The next year, as his team's quarterback, he led Notre Dame through an undefeated season to the championship. He was voted the Heisman trophy winner, and signed a $300,000 bonus contract with the New York Jets. Had he learned how to be successful!

Sure, but he was born with exceptional talent, you say. Well, how about George Mikan? As a sophomore at Joliet (Illinois) High School, he showed up at the gym to try out for the basketball team. The coach threw him the ball — Mikan wasn't even coordinated enough to catch it! He had determination though; he made the extraordinary investment in hours and effort to develop what a champion needs to have.

The results: Mikan was a three-year all-American at LaSalle and later played twelve years for the Minnesota

Lakers. At Minnesota he received the National Basketball Association's outstanding player award.

Tuckett believes the main reason more people do not make the investment and become as great as they could be is the fear of failure. "It is the greatest 'de-motivator' there is," he claims. "Fear is a paralyzing thing." Fear immobilizes you so you cannot do what you need to do. Tuckett offers some suggestions for overcoming the fear of failure.

First, expect a certain natural percentage of nonsuccess experiences in your efforts. No one is completely successful all the time. This is where those who have big numbers investment have the advantage over those who do not. If you try ten times more than anyone else, you can afford to fail many times and still end up a super success.

Two sales representatives for Lear Jet Corporation might be able to sell one of their classy planes to one prospect out of every five hundred contacts. (These figures are purely speculative.) If one salesman is afraid of being turned down, so he falteringly talks to only five hundred people during a year, he will only sell one jet. (Incidentally, he probably won't be a salesman for long.)

If the other salesman expects a certain number of rejections and does not allow himself to be frozen by worry, he may enthusiastically contact several thousand prospects and sell eight planes in a year. This is a direct example of the law of probability, easily seen, yet the first man's potential for success was strangled by his fear of failure.

Second, cultivate the awareness that even great men fail. Tuckett goes beyond this, in fact. He has noticed that the men who have contributed most to the world were also "the world's most proficient failures."

George Washington, for example, had some abysmal failures as a general. Abraham Lincoln ran for political office over and over, but the gangly lawyer was repeatedly defeated. A list of his losses is impressive indeed.

Babe Ruth held the world's record for home runs, until Mickey Mantle came along. Babe was and still is loved and revered by thousands. Scarcely anyone remembers that Babe Ruth also struck out more times than any other batter in the history of baseball.

The St. Louis Cardinal basestealing champ, Lou Brock, has successfully stolen an incredible 118 bases. The crowd roars with delight when he picks off another one. Yet a scrutiny of the records tells us that Brock has been thrown out thirty-three times! Another record! He failed thirty-three times. Thirty-three times Lou Brock made his way back to the dugout knowing he had failed, knowing that even if the next batter hit a home run he (Brock) could not add a run to his team's score by crossing home plate.

It is obvious that a sometime failure does not automatically dump a person into a pile of misfits and undesirables. On the contrary, virtually all of the world's greatest are counted among those who have failed.

Do not be afraid to try for fear of failing. Instead, force yourself to try more times. Remember: It's a numbers game!

Third, it helps to keep in mind that "failure is the ignition to all greatness," as Tuckett puts it. If you were successful at everything you tried, your life would be a shallow satisfaction. You would never develop the resiliency, perseverance, character, and deep satisfaction that grow through the constant effort to improve and adapt.

Paul Ehrlich's name is not widely known in our time. Yet this man exemplifies recurring effort in the face of defeat. A German bacteriologist and immunologist, he was determined to find a way to combine several elements with arsenic. Ehrlich combined the elements in every combination and under every condition he could think of. In fact, he varied his experiment 605 unsuccessful times! The 606th time he succeeded.

The resulting substance was marketed under the appropriate title of "606". Chemically, it was arsphenamine. Later trademarked Salvarsan, "606" became the specific cure for the dreaded syphilis. What an enormous numbers investment this Nobel prizewinner made in his experiments, failing often and learning from his mistakes until he inevitably accomplished his goal.

Glenn loves to pluck these interesting but little-known stories about champs from the obscurity of old records. George Mikan, Johnny Huart, Babe Ruth, Lou Brock, Washington, Lincoln, Paul Ehrlich — each man's story is an example that others can learn to be successful if they will learn the success rules. The fear of failure is the main reason most people never learn.

Once the fear of failure has been dealt with, anyone who successfully uses the principle of "greater investment equals greater returns" must be willing to work. To put it another way, "The only thing that stands between some people and the top of the ladder is the ladder."

Tuckett points out that a hundred years ago, most of man's work was done by sheer muscle power. Today technology has changed all that. Appliances do everything for us. Some people never learn the lessons of work and discipline that the physical nature of our forebears' lives automatically taught them. "If we don't watch out, we're going to completely lose the privilege of working," he says, "and it is a privilege, not a curse.

"I'd prefer to have farm boys show up for my teams," he says. "They're used to doing chores, and they know how to work. I send some of the other guys out to the field to work out, and they don't know what I mean."

Of course, response to our technological world is a

matter of outlook. The ten percent who "have memorized every excuse there is for losing" may continue to get by. They will do as little as possible on a boring assembly line job and spend their evenings watching other people "really" live on TV.

Look back at any of the success examples used here and it is clear he was willing to work hard in order to achieve greatness in his field. These winners will find numerous opportunities to get more and more done. In fact, they will find all kinds of mechanical aids to help them be more efficient in their work.

Given an understanding of the numbers game, the control of fear, and a willingness to work, it simply remains to discover the most innovative and workable ways of putting numbers to work for you. It's a matter of running around versus creative thinking.

Time is precious. No successful person wants to spend his day doing something ineffective when he can pack it with vital, useful, productive activity.

Different types of problems are helped by variations of the numbers game. Asking "How can I get this job done in less time?" can stimulate creative solutions to problems

In the real estate field, simple numbers do not bring success. Few buy the first property they see. This is even truer of the investment buyer in search of a super deal. You need to look at dozens of properties, compare the possibilities, their histories, financing, etc.

Once you are conscious of the numbers game you will see its implications in all areas of life, even in emotions and human ties. Speaking of personal relationships, Max Gunther says in his book *The Luck Factor* that the luckiest people are usually those who form many friendships. They go out of their way to strike up conversations, to learn about the lives of their acquaintances, and to become friendly with people who fascinate them.

By taking every chance to get to know interesting people, lives can be enriched and many doors opened. On the other hand, fearful people who have impoverished social lives rarely turn out to be successes.

There are countless facets to life. Each person wants success in his own individual way. No two people want exactly the same thing out of life. Choose your field. Set your goals. Decide what *you* want to accomplish. Tuckett says, "The greater the dedication and commitment we have, the harder it is to surrender."

Use the numbers laws creatively to accomplish your goals in the fastest and best way possible. Anyone can do what he really wants to do. It is possible to pack more living (enjoyable, fulfilled, and pleasant living) into fewer days, and in essence live a much longer life.

That is what it's all about. Man was meant to succeed. You, too, can put the laws of probability to work to enrich your life, as champions in every field have done. Says Glenn Tuckett, expressing the feelings of most of us, "These are the kinds of guys that are enshrined in my own private Hall of Fame."

NOTES AND THOUGHTS

CHAPTER 19

A TAX TALE OF TWO FAMILIES

I'd like you to meet Mr. and Mrs. Worker, a nice couple with two children. Both he and she work and earn $40,000 between them. Their income is augmented by $525 they earn at 5½ percent annual interest on a $10,000 savings account. So their total annual income is $40,525.

With the revision in the tax laws boosting the personal exemption to $1,000 per individual, and with the standard deduction for a couple being $3,400, Mr. and Mrs. Worker can deduct a family total of $7,400 making their taxable income $33,125. (For this example we are excluding other deductions they may be entitled to such as interest, medical expenses, contributions, etc.)

Now, like most Americans, when Mr. and Mrs. Worker collect their paycheck, it shows that the Internal Revenue Service (IRS) beat them to their money and took a tax bite. By the end of the year they have had about $8,000 withheld for taxes.

However, at year's end, their actual, computed tax is only (only?) $6,630 so they receive an IRS refund of $1,370*. (See TABLE I.)

Let's meet another couple, Mr. and Mrs. Investor.

Like Mr. and Mrs. Worker, they have two children, their salaries total $40,000, they had $8,000 withheld for taxes, and they had $10,000 in savings. *But* . . .

Realizing that their savings were being eaten up by inflation — and the interest was being taxed as ordinary income — they withdrew their $10,000, borrowed another $10,000, and invested the total $20,000 as down payment on a $200,000 apartment building.

*Note: Tax Schedule for 1982 according to new Tax Act of 1981.

TABLE I

Salary income	$40,000
Five ¼ percent interest on $10,000 savings	525
Total annual income	40,525
Personal exemptions at $1,000 each	4,000
Standard deduction for family	3,400
Taxable income	$33,125
Taxes withheld from salary	$8,000
Actual, computed tax on 33,125	6,630
Refund from IRS	$1,370

Bottom line:	Total income	$40,525
	Total Tax	6,630
	Refund check from IRS	$1,370

TABLE II

Salary income	$40,000
Personal exemptions at $1,000 each and the standard deduction	7,400
Taxable income	32,600
Schedule E deductions (for income property)	28,168
Final taxable income	$ 4,432
Taxes withheld from salary	$ 8,000
Less actual computed tax (on $4,432)	124
Total IRS refund	$ 7,876

Not having the five and one-fourth percent interest income from their savings any more lowered their annual, personal income to $40,000. Their standard deduction and personal exemptions were $7,400 leaving their taxable income at $32,600.

However, with an income property they compute their taxes on the Internal Revenue Services' "Schedule E" form.

Under "Schedule E", they can deduct $28,168 from their taxable income. Where did that $28,168 come from? A good question. But just put it on "hold" and we'll give the answer further on.

As you can see in TABLE II, when you deduct $28,168 from their personal, taxable income of $32,600, that latter figure is reduced to $4,432.

But remember, they had $8,000 withheld from their paychecks. If you take the computed tax on $4,432 of $124 from the $8,000 withheld, you can see that Mr. and Mrs. Investor have a nice refund of $7,876.

Isn't that terrific!

That's $7,876 cash-in-hand to reinvest or do with as they will. (As *Financial Freedom Report* subscribers they'll probably reinvest it.)

But let's move on to that interesting looking $28,168 that you want to know about; let's get down to the nitty-gritty.

To find the $28,168, we need to understand the tax benefits that come with the ownership of income property.

Let's take a look at the economics of the property shown in TABLE III. From actual experience, we can say that a $200,000 rental property can generate a $34,000 annual income — that figure will vary from one area of the country to another depending upon local rent structures and vacancy factors, but more importantly upon how well the property is geared for *optimum* rents.

TABLE III

Annual income from rentals		$34,000
Interest expense on borrowed		
$10,000 and $180,000 mortgage	$17,200	
Building operating expenses	12,800	30,000
Gross profit		4,000
Payment on $10,000 and $180,000 principal		3,000
Total net profit		$ 1,000

TABLE IV

Annual income from rentals	$34,000
Interest and operating expenses	30,000
Gross profit	4,000
Depreciation	32,168
Net loss	$28,168

As TABLE III shows, from the $34,000, Mr. and Mrs. Investor would deduct $30,000 for interest payments and operating costs. (That $30,000 is comprised of $17,200 to pay the interest figured on the borrowed $10,000 and on the $180,000 mortgage; and $12,800 for operating expenses including such things as some utilities, replacing drapes and carpeting, painting and general upkeep.)

Deducting the $30,000 in expenses from their $34,000 rental income leaves a gross profit of $4,000.

From the $4,000 they make $3,000 principal payments on the $10,000 and the $180,000.

This leaves a net profit for Mr. and Mrs. Investor of $1,000.

Hey, wait a minute! If Mr. and Mrs. Investor make a net *profit* of $1,000, how can they claim a *loss* of $28,168 on their income tax return?

How? Depreciation!

But, you may ask, how can something depreciate in value when in fact the market value is increasing? The answer to that is one of the beauties of the U.S. tax laws. It's there in black and white.

Probably the whole thing started when some businessman went to Uncle Sam and said, "Hey, the truck I bought two years ago is wearing out; it's depreciating in value. Can't I claim that as a business expense and deduct the amount from my taxes?"

"Well, OK," said Uncle Sam, and he passed a law making it so.

It seemed such a good idea to a lot of people, including rental property owners who probably complained to Uncle Sam that their buildings were depreciating from wear and tear. "And what about all the stuff inside," they asked. "That's depreciating too, you know."

It seemed that Uncle Sam agreed that all this wear and tear, and that all the depreciation could be classified as a business expense, and the laws were adjusted to reflect that decision.

And that is how Mr. and Mrs. Investors' $1,000 net *profit* changed into a handsome $28,168 tax write-off.

Briefly, let's review some of our figures. (See TABLE IV.)

We had an annual rental income of $34,000 less interest and operating expenses, leaving a gross profit of $4,000.

Now we feed in a *depreciation* figure of $32,168 for a net loss of $28,168.

That's where the $28,168 comes from.

But, you ask, where did the $32,168 come from?

Walk through the figures in TABLE V.

Let's figure the depreciation.

First, the land on which the structure stands.

How do you calculate the depreciation of land, if it can be done at all? It can't. Therefore, owners need to deduct (as a rule-of-thumb) at least a ten percent land value factor from the purchase price of the property before calculating depreciation on the building.

For tax purposes, this means that Mr. and Mrs. Investor's property automatically depreciated by ten percent, or $20,000 to $180,000.

From the $180,000 they then deduct the depreciation for the contents of the building.

For example, in a building of this size, the furniture and furnishings (drapes, carpets, etc.) could easily be valued at $40,000. Uncle Sam says that furniture can be depreciated over three years, or, in this case, $13,335 per year.

TABLE V

Property	$200,000
Minus ten percent factor for land value	20,000
Value of structure and contents	180,000
Minus attributed depreciation value of furnishings	40,000
	$140,000
Minus attributed depreciation value of equipment	30,000
	$110,000

Value of furniture, furnishings
  (3-year life) $ 40,000   or $13,335 per year for 3 years

Value of equipment
  (5-year life)   30,000   or   6,000 per year for 5 years

Structure (15 years*)
  [using accelerated 175%
  depreciation]   110,000   or   12,833 per year for first year

Annual tax write-off
    for the first year = $32,168

TABLE VI

For $20,000 invested in down payment	$ 1,000 cash flow	or	5%
At a given inflation rate of 6% during first year	12,000	or	60% (on original $20,000 invested)
Tax savings ($7,876 less $1,370 they would have received as per Table I)	6,506	or	33%
Equity built-up by payments on mortgage (paid from rental income)	3,000	or	15%
Return on investment			113% (in first year)

*New 1981 Tax Act; Accelerated Cost Recovery System

Next is the equipment in the building such as air conditioners, the furnace, the kitchen and utility room appliances. These can be depreciated over five years, or $6,000 per year.

Uncle Sam says that the structure itself can be depreciated over fifteen years.* However, the depreciation rate can be accelerated by one hundred and twenty-five percent. In this case it means an annual tax write-off of $12,833 for the first year.

When you add up the tax write-offs you find the $32,168.

That's Mr. and Mrs. Investor's annual tax write-off for the first year.

Of course, after three years, the write-off is minus the depreciation deduction for furniture and furnishings, and after another two years, Mr. and Mrs. Investor lose the depreciation deduction on the equipment. But for another ten years they continue to have the depreciation on the building itself.

TABLE VI is very interesting. It shows the total return on Mr. and Mrs. Investor's invested dollar of 113 percent. Not bad for these days.

This is calculated at a given inflation rate of six percent. (Most times it's higher.) Even without the inflation factor, the return on their investment is a very comfortable fifty-three percent.

As you can see, starting with the same economic base as Mr. and Mrs. Worker, Mr. and Mrs. Investor found themselves a pretty solid investment with a fantastic return, tremendous tax savings through depreciation, and extra cash . . . through the ownership of income property.

---

*Note: For properties placed into service after Decembere 31, 1980 the 1981 Tax Act Accelerated Cost Recovery System applies. (15 year "life" 175% accelerated method.)

NOTES AND THOUGHTS

CHAPTER 20

HOW TO MAKE YOUR DOLLAR WORK HARDER FOR YOU

Where will our money work the hardest? Where can we consistently receive the highest rate of return?

In today's world, the answer to that question is real estate. By making wise purchases and by using leverage, a person can make a million dollars in a relatively small amount of time with real estate.

Real estate is *the* money-making approach — but it works only for those who are willing to take action. We all have a friend who says, "You know that property up on Third Street? The one with the old six-unit flat on it? Why, I could have bought that four years ago for $31,000 and now it's worth nearly $100,000!"

Our friend is right, of course. But he isn't rich. He failed to *act* on the opportunity when it presented itself. None of us can make any money from opportunities that have passed and gone.

But there are plenty of people who *did* act, who have made their fortune through wise real estate investments. Even now, hundreds of thousands of people are getting rich from properties they own.

Why is real estate such a good investment? Why do experts predict that the real estate market may slow down but will probably never fail?

Real estate is a basic need. People always need a place to live, a place to work, a place to farm. Improved real estate is especially in demand — apartment units, single family houses, duplexes, and the like.

Each kind of real estate has its own unique characteristics. Each has different risks and rewards. Of all the different types of real estate available, I am biased toward rental units, either apartments or single family homes. They are such a basic need that it's hard to go wrong with them. Naturally, you have to buy right with any kind of real estate, and use utmost care in the management of the property but — apartments are in short supply and rents are constantly going up.

I made my first million with rental units.

But if you don't like rentals, there are plenty of other ways you can get rich with real estate. You can put your money in everything from farm land as an investment to recreational land for development and future speculation. You can buy such income-producing properties as shopping centers, apartment buildings, office buildings, medical complexes, hotels, motels, or industrial buildings. Or you might want to create condominiums by purchasing apartment buildings and converting from a rental situation to a sale situation, selling each unit individually.

Whether you decide to get into apartments or some other form of real estate, though, you'll find it difficult to fail.

But how does one get started? I remember the hard time I had taking that first step. Part of the problem is fear; part of it is inexperience. I remember how I worried about losing money through vacancies; how I worried about all my tenants moving out at once. What if the furnace stopped working? I wondered. What if the roof started leaking? Will the value of real estate continue to rise? Will I be able to meet my payments?

These worries and fears kept me from doing anything for almost a year. That year cost me many thousands of dollars.

But finally I made up my mind to move ahead and not look back. I'm glad I did. My wealth has grown.

There are many ways to buy real estate. Usually, the greater the leverage the greater the profits. That usually means income properties that are bought for low or no down payments.

Other than leverage, one thing that can help the careful investor is the fact that real estate is an imperfect market. It is unique in that there is no one central place of exchange where all properties are bought and sold. You could pay $50,000 for a four-unit apartment building that sits right next door to a four-unit apartment building that I paid $80,000 for. And they could be identical in every respect. There are many reasons for this discrepancy: the seller may not have gone to the trouble of getting an appraisal; he may have paid $20,000 and would be absolutely delighted to get $50,000 for the property. The seller may need to unload the property fast — he may be divorced, or need cash, or may be fed up, or moving out of the area.

Whatever the reason for the difference in price, the smart investor has much to gain by shopping around for bargains. If he is persistent, he will eventually find a property that is listed far below the market value.

But looking around for properties takes a lot of time, and most of us don't have a lot of time. I don't have a lot of time, so I developed a method whereby I can find the bargains without a major expenditure of that commodity.

I call it the shotgun method, because it goes off in all directions like a shotgun does. Here's how the method works:

First, I go through the multiple-listing book for the area that I'm interested in. These books are available for almost any city in the United States. I look in the book for the kinds of properties that I would be interested in. I mark

down all those that look promising. That is, if I want four-
or five-unit apartment dwelling, I look only at those, and
mark down only those.

It usually takes about two hours to go through the entire book. I am able to come up with anything from a
dozen to five dozen potential properties.

Next, I make offers on dozens of the properties that I
listed, offering the owner twenty, thirty, or even forty percent less than he listed the property for.

The offer I usually make up is fairly standard. An offer on a $60,000 piece of property might read like this:

"Offer Price: $48,000
"Down payment: $4,000
"Seller to carry contract on balance for thirty years at
nine and-a-half percent. This offer is subject to the buyer
inspecting the physical premises and accepting the same."

If I think the seller needs cash I may put in a balloon
payment. That is, the contract balance would all be due
and payable after say, the tenth year. This gets my monthly payment down low, and, of course, I figure I can
either sell the place or get refinancing within ten years.

I also include in the offer the size of the monthly payment, an agreement on who will pay taxes and insurance,
and all the other small details that are normally contained
in the standard purchase offer form.

In the next step, I call in one or more real estate
agents, give them the offer and the earnest money, and ask
them to handle the deal. They take the offers to the sellers
and try to convince them to accept my terms.

As you would imagine, most offers come back "not
accepted." Out of thirty offers, normally twenty-five will
not be accepted. But on the remaining five a counter-offer
will be made, usually at a price somewhere between my of-

fering price and the seller's original price.

And occasionally, much to my delight, the original offer is accepted.

Finally, I go to inspect each of the properties that seems to have the right price. If I like it, I can proceed with the closing. If I don't like, I am not bound to continue, even if my original offer was accepted. Remember, the offer was "subject to the buyer inspecting the physical premises and accepting the same."

This method multiplies your effectiveness many times. With this approach, you can make hundreds of offers in a short period of time, and you can quickly find which sellers are motivated to sell their properties for low prices.

Using this method, I was able to purchase over twenty-four properties in only a matter of months. I did it virtually by myself, using only brokers and agents to present the offers. Many of the deals were well under true market price, and I was thereby able to catapult my net worth into hundreds of thousands of dollars in a very short time.

I sincerely hope what you have learned or re-learned from reading this book will help catapult you to your own financial goals—I know it possible—it will work but only if you do. The road to riches is simple but not easy—it takes effort and discipline—were it not so, beggars, winos and bums would all be millionaires.

But believe me developing your own potential through discipline is well worth effort. What's more the rewards are much more than the great financial rewards you'll receive. So be a tough taskmaster on yourself and you'll not only acquire a vast estate for your own security and your families but you'll vastly improve yourself as an individual and productive human being contributing to the wealth of others. I guarantee you'll find as much or more satisfaction in that than in the money.

I hope you and I will meet someday—maybe at one of our many seminars. For information on a seminar or convention nearest you call my office at 1-801-943-1280.

Now if you want to really implant the material you have just read deeply in your mind and memory bank may I suggest the Financial Genius tapes, which are available by calling the same phone number or writing to Financial Genius Tapes, Dept. CT-009, 1831 Fort Union Blvd., Salt Lake City, Utah 84121.

These tapes explain in detail every single chapter and paragraph of the Financial Genius Book (1980 edition) with plenty of updating comments for todays market.

Best wishes to you in all your endeavors, financial and otherwise.

Notes And Thoughts

APPENDIX A

Compound Tables
(Based on beginning capital of $10,000)

Years	5%	15%	25%	30%
1	10,050	11,500	12,500	13,000
2	11,025	13,225	15,625	16,900
3	11,576	15,208	19,531	21,970
4	12,155	17,490	24,414	28,561
5	12,762	20,113	30,517	37,129
6	13,400	23,130	38,146	48,268
7	14,071	26,600	47,683	62,748
8	14,774	30,590	59,604	81,573
9	15,513	35,178	74,505	106,044
10	16,288	40,455	93,132	137,858
11	17,103	46,523	116,415	179,211
12	17,958	53,502	145,519	232,980
13	18,856	61,527	181,898	302,875
14	19,799	70,757	227,373	393,737
15	20,789	81,370	284,217	511,858
16	21,828	93,576	355,271	665,416
17	22,920	107,612	444,089	865,041
18	24,066	123,754	555,111	1,124,554
19	25,269	142,317	693,889	1,461,920
20	26,532	163,665	867,361	1,900,496
21	27,859	188,215	1,084,202	2,470,645
22	29,252	216,447	1,355,252	3,211,838
23	30,715	248,914	1,694,065	4,174,390
24	32,251	286,251	2,117,582	5,428,007
25	33,863	329,189	2,646,977	7,056,409

APPENDIX A

Compound Tables
(Based on beginning capital of $10,000)

Years	50%	100%
1	15,000	20,000
2	22,500	40,000
3	33,750	80,000
4	50,625	160,000
5	75,938	320,000
6	113,907	640,000
7	170,860	1,280,000
8	256,290	2,560,000
9	384,435	5,120,000
10	576,635	10,240,000
11	864,979	20,480,000
12	1,297,468	40,960,000
13	1,946,201	81,920,000
14	2,919,303	163,840,000
15	4,378,954	327,680,000
16	6,568,431	655,360,000
17	9,852,651	1,310,720,000
18	14,778,976	2,621,440,000
19	22,168,464	5,242,880,000
20	33,252,696	10,485,760,000
21	49,879,044	20,971,520,000
22	74,818,566	41,943,040,000
23	112,227,849	83,886,080,000
24	168,341,779	167,772,160,000
25	252,512,668	335,544,320,000

$10,000 at 30% Compounded 18 Years

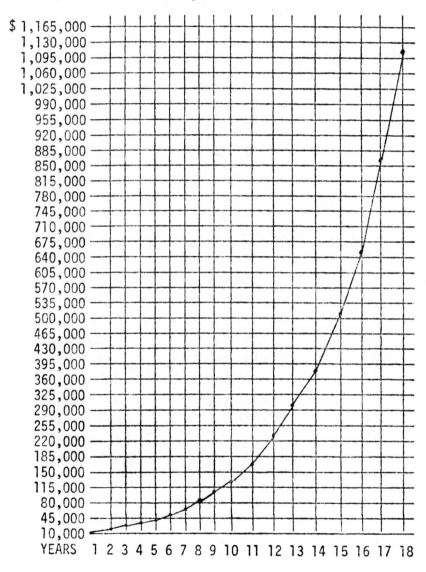

Outlook by States

(Based on U.S. Census Bureau population projections for 1990)

	1970 population	Under lowest projection		Under highest projection	
		1990 population	Change from 1970	1990 population	Change from 1970
Alabama	3,444,000	3,692,000	Up 7.2%	4,435,000	Up 28.8%
Alaska	300,000	392,000	Up 30.7%	491,000	Up 63.7%
Arizona	1,771,000	2,375,000	Up 34.1%	2,724,000	Up 53.8%
Arkansas	1,923,000	2,195,000	Up 14.1%	2,515,000	Up 30.8%
California	19,953,000	25,851,000	Up 29.6%	30,528,000	Up 53.0%
Colorado	2,207,000	2,730,000	Up 23.7%	3,268,000	Up 48.1%
Connecticut	3,032,000	3,774,000	Up 24.5%	4,377,000	Up 44.4%
Delaware	548,000	687,000	Up 25.4%	818,000	Up 49.3%
Florida	6,789,000	7,805,000	Up 15.0%	10,241,000	Up 50.8%
Georgia	4,590,000	5,698,000	Up 24.1%	6,204,000	Up 35.2%
Hawaii	769,000	933,000	Up 21.3%	1,245,000	Up 61.9%
Idaho	713,000	817,000	Up 14.6%	979,000	Up 37.3%
Illinois	11,114,000	13,464,000	Up 21.1%	14,740,000	Up 32.6%
Indiana	5,194,000	6,354,000	Up 22.3%	6,852,000	Up 31.9%
Iowa	2,824,000	3,009,000	Up 6.6%	3,629,000	Up 28.5%
Kansas	2,247,000	2,432,000	Up 8.2%	2,828,000	Up 25.9%
Kentucky	3,219,000	3,540,000	Up 10.0%	4,144,000	Up 28.7%
Louisiana	3,641,000	4,285,000	Up 17.7%	5,104,000	Up 40.2%
Maine	992,000	1,044,000	Up 5.2%	1,316,000	Up 32.7%
Maryland	3,922,000	4,821,000	Up 22.9%	6,068,000	Up 54.7%
Massachusetts	5,689,000	6,869,000	Up 20.7%	7,542,000	Up 32.6%
Michigan	8,875,000	11,193,000	Up 26.1%	12,051,000	Up 35.8%
Minnesota	3,805,000	4,703,000	Up 23.6%	5,175,000	Up 36.0%
Mississippi	2,217,000	2,288,000	Up 3.2%	3,075,000	Up 38.7%
Missouri	4,677,000	5,410,000	Up 15.7%	5,887,000	Up 25.9%
Montana	694,000	757,000	Up 9.1%	943,000	Up 35.9%
Nebraska	1,483,000	1,664,000	Up 12.2%	1,942,000	Up 31.0%
Nevada	489,000	629,000	Up 28.6%	903,000	Up 84.7%
New Hampshire	738,000	900,000	Up 22.0%	1,096,000	Up 48.5%
New Jersey	7,168,000	8,694,000	Up 21.3%	10,152,000	Up 41.6%
New Mexico	1,016,000	1,160,000	Up 14.2%	1,608,000	Up 58.3%
New York	18,191,000	21,461,000	Up 18.0%	24,702,000	Up 35.8%
North Carolina	5,082,000	5,852,000	Up 15.2%	6,510,000	Up 28.1%
North Dakota	618,000	594,000	Down 3.9%	864,000	Up 39.8%
Ohio	10,652,000	12,693,000	Up 19.2%	13,764,000	Up 29.2%
Oklahoma	2,559,000	2,941,000	Up 14.9%	3,245,000	Up 26.8%
Oregon	2,091,000	2,425,000	Up 16.0%	2,940,000	Up 40.6%
Pennsylvania	11,794,000	12,529,000	Up 6.2%	14,110,000	Up 19.6%
Rhode Island	947,000	1,104,000	Up 16.6%	1,248,000	Up 31.8%
South Carolina	2,591,000	2,855,000	Up 10.2%	3,454,000	Up 33.3%
South Dakota	666,000	662,000	Down 0.6%	915,000	Up 37.4%
Tennessee	3,924,000	4,575,000	Up 16.6%	4,903,000	Up 24.9%
Texas	11,197,000	14,358,000	Up 28.2%	15,640,000	Up 39.7%
Utah	1,059,000	1,400,000	Up 32.2%	1,645,000	Up 55.3%
Vermont	444,000	549,000	Up 23.6%	605,000	Up 36.3%
Virginia	4,648,000	5,603,000	Up 20.5%	6,179,000	Up 32.9%
Washington	3,409,000	4,116,000	Up 20.7%	4,810,000	Up 41.1%
West Virginia	1,744,000	1,565,000	Down 10.3%	2,095,000	Up 20.1%
Wisconsin	4,418,000	5,466,000	Up 23.7%	5,913,000	Up 33.8%
Wyoming	332,000	360,000	Up 8.4%	450,000	Up 35.5%

Note: Low projections assume relatively low fertility rates and generally unfavorable trends of migration for each State. High projections assume a higher fertility rate and more favorable migration trends.

Census Bureau says "reasonable" projections for District of Columbia not available.